The Right of Privacy in the Computer Age

Recent Titles from Quorum Books

Evaluating Corporate Investment and Financing Opportunities: A Handbook and Guide to Selected Methods for Managers and Finance Professionals
Sherman L. Lewis

Handbook of Management Control Systems
Ahmed Belkaoui

Currency Fluctuations and the Perception of Corporate Performance: A Communications Approach to Financial Accounting and Reporting
Loretta Graziano

International Law of Take-Overs and Mergers: United States, Canada, and South and Central America
H. Leigh Ffrench

The Foreign Debt/National Development Conflict: External Adjustment and Internal Disorder in the Developing Nations
Chris C. Carvounis

Effective Financial Management in Public and Nonprofit Agencies: A Practical and Integrative Approach
Jerome B. McKinney

The Logic of Intuitive Decision Making: A Research-Based Approach for Top Management
Weston H. Agor

International Law of Take-Overs and Mergers: The EEC, Northern Europe, and Scandinavia
H. Leigh Ffrench

Office Information Technology: A Decision-Maker's Guide to Systems Planning and Implementation
Randy J. Goldfield

Developing a Professional Sales Force: A Guide for Sales Trainers and Sales Managers
David A. Stumm

A Working Guide for Directors of Not-for-Profit Organizations
Charles N. Waldo

Causation, Prediction, and Legal Analysis
Stuart S. Nagel

The Right of Privacy in the Computer Age

Warren Freedman

Q
Quorum Books
NEW YORK • WESTPORT, CONNECTICUT • LONDON

Library of Congress Cataloging-in-Publication Data

Freedman, Warren.
The right of privacy in the computer age.

Bibliography: p.
Includes index.
1. Privacy, Right of. 2. Computers—Access control.
I. Title.
JC596.F74 1987 323.44'8 86-9362
ISBN 0-89930-187-8 (lib. bdg. : alk. paper)

Library of Congress Catalog Card Number: 86-9362
ISBN: 0-89930-187-8

First published in 1987 by Quorum Books

Greenwood Press, Inc.
88 Post Road West, Westport, Connecticut 06881

Printed in the United States of America

The paper used in this book complies with the Permanent Paper Standard issued by the National Information Standards Organization (Z39.48-1984).

10 9 8 7 6 5 4 3 2 1

Contents

Preface

The right of privacy looms more and more important day by day in this computer age as the impact of scientific progress dawns upon society. The coverage of the subject matter in this volume embracing six chapters does not bog down with esoteric philosophical or social discussion; nor is the volume overwhelmingly concerned with the historical development of the right of privacy. What the author seeks is a realistic delineation of the substance and the parameters of the right of privacy; he is ever aware of the need of judicial and pragmatic relief from invasions, intrusions, or interferences with the right of privacy in the present-day world. Chapter One is a general treatment of the subject matter, although it encompasses the New York Law of Privacy, the "right of publicity," and in § 1.10 the very basic elements of the cause of action.

Chapter Two is devoted to examples of intrusion, invasion, or interference, not only with respect to kind or types but with respect to specific tortfeasance in selected situations. The constitutional basis for the right of privacy is delineated in Chapter Three with emphasis upon the First and Fourth Amendments to the U.S. Constitution. Chapter Four analyzes various modern techniques and current operations that infringe upon the right of privacy; and Chapter Five deals specifically with judicial remedies, which include compensatory and punitive damages and criminal penalties. The international aspects are set forth in Chapter Six, highlighting Europe, Israel, and the Soviet Union. (The Appendix provides the Israel Protection of Privacy Bill.)

The reader, whether a practicing attorney, a law professor, a business person, or a student, will find this single volume to be a welcome addition to his or her library. The book reads easily, is devoid of excessive legalism, and provides what an intelligent and curious person needs to know about the right of privacy. In the words of Adlai E. Stevenson of Illinois, "You are a child of the universe no less than the trees and the stars, you have a right to be here."

The Right of Privacy in the Computer Age

1

Definition and Historical Framework of the Right of Privacy

1.1 ORIGINS AND HISTORICAL BACKGROUND

It was in the year 1890 in the city of Boston that Professors Louis D. Brandeis and Samuel D. Warren pondered over the undue newspaper publicity given to the private social affairs of Mrs. Warren. These Harvard Law School professors thereupon in December 1890 published in Volume 4 of the *Harvard Law Review* (beginning at page 193) an impassioned indictment of the "yellow journalism" of their day. Their endorsement of a right to recover for "invasion of privacy" was geared to criticism of the press:

> The press is overstepping in every direction the obvious bounds of propriety and of decency. Gossip is no longer the resource of the idle and of the vicious, but has become a trade, which is pursued with industry as well as effrontery. To satisfy a prurient taste the details of sexual relations are spread broadcast in the columns of the daily papers. To occupy the indolent, column upon column is filled with idle gossip, which can only be procured by intrusion upon the domestic circle. The intensity and complexity of life, attendant upon advancing civilization, have rendered necessary some retreat from the world, and man, under the refining influence of culture, has become more sensitive to publicity, so that solitude and privacy have become more essential to the individual; but modern enterprise and invention have, through invasions upon his privacy, subjected him to mental pain and distress, far greater than could be inflicted by mere bodily injury.

It was from such humble origins that the right of privacy, synthesized from common law cases as a right of each individual to determine "ordinarily, to what extent his thoughts, sentiments, and emotions shall be communicated to others'' (p. 198), was created. The Brandeis and Warren *Law Review* article was a remarkable essay and for the past ninety-six years has been widely quoted by lawyers, judges, social psychologists, and sociologists, in particular. The following excerpts are worthy of note:

[T]he right to life has come to mean the right to enjoy life—the right to be let alone. . . . Recent inventions and business methods call attention to the next step which must be taken for the protection of the person. . . .

The common law secures to each individual the right of determining, ordinarily, to what extent his thoughts, sentiments, and emotions shall be communicated to others. . . . The existence of this right does not depend upon the particular method of expression adopted. . . . Neither does the existence of the right depend upon the nature or value of the thought or emotion, nor upon the excellence of the means of expression. . . . In every case, the individual is entitled to decide whether that which is his shall be given to the public. . . .

A man records in a letter to his son, or in his diary, that he did not dine with his wife on a certain day. No one into whose hands those papers fall could publish them to the world. . . . What is the thing which is protected? Surely, not the intellectual act of recording the fact that the husband did not dine with his wife, but that fact itself. . . .

If privacy is once recognized as a right entitled to legal protection, the interposition of the courts cannot depend upon the particular nature of the injuries resulting. . . . It is like the right not to be assaulted or beaten, the right not to be imprisoned, the right not to be maliciously prosecuted, the right not to be defamed. . . . there inheres the quality of being owned or possessed . . . as property. . . . The principle which protects . . . is in reality not the principle of private property, but that of an inviolate personality.

The rights, so protected, whatever their exact nature, are not rights arising from contract or from special trust, but are rights against the world. . . . If the invasion of privacy constitutes legal injuria, the elements for demanding redress exist, since already the value of mental suffering, caused by an act wrongful in itself, is recognized as a basis for compensation. . . .

The right to privacy does not prohibit any publication of matter which is of public general interest. . . .

The right of privacy does not prohibit the communication of any matter though in its nature private, when the publication is made under circumstances which would render it a privileged communication according to the law of libel and slander. . . .

The law would probably not grant any redress for the invasion of privacy by oral publication in the absence of special damage. . . .

The right of privacy eases upon the publication of the facts by the individual or with his consent. . . .

The truth of the matter published does not afford a defense. . . . The absence of ''malice'' in the publisher does not afford a defense. . . .

It would appear that Professors Brandeis and Warren were principally concerned not with a broad right to be let alone but rather with the right to protect oneself from having one's private affairs known to others and to keep secret intimate facts about oneself from the prying eyes or ears of other persons. In the pre-1890 pioneer society an individual's privacy was not in danger of serious encroachment, and so there was little need to protect his so-called right to enjoy life. But the post-1890 industrial society and the complexity of the twentieth century have changed the situation materially, and today it is very difficult to live a peaceful and quiet existence. The recognition of a right of privacy is one aspect of a growing body of law designed to protect the individual from interference with his peace of mind. But the loss of financial interest associated in many cases with recognition of the right of privacy must be balanced against society's requirement of free speech and dissemination of the truth about people and things.

Probably the earliest intimation of a *legal* right of privacy is found in Jewish law. The Mishna (dated about the year 200) explains that "if one builds a wall opposite his fellow's windows, whether it is higher or lower than them, it may not be within four cubits" (Baba Batra II, 4). The thrust of the Mishna division of the Talmud is that a person should not peer and look into another's house. The great Jewish scholar, physician, astrologist, and writer Maimonides declared in the year 1180 that "the harm of being seen in privacy is a legal wrong" (Mishna Torah, Neighbors II, 14). The Romans recognized privacy in their word *iniuria*, which included the willful disregard of another's personality; and the Greeks by *contumelia* meant an infringement of the personality of another.

It was not until the year 1818, in Gee v. Pritchard (36 Eng Rep 670), that English law restrained the publication of a private letter as a court of chancery took that unusual step to protect a "property right." Seven years later, in 1825, in Abernethey v. Hutchinson (47 Eng Rep 1313) a court of chancery restrained the publication for profit by a medical student of the lectures of a teaching surgeon. But these English cases based their protection of the right of privacy upon the protection of a "property right." Indeed, the early view of privacy was directly linked to a property standard and not related to the more modern concept of "liberty." Even in the United States the earliest level of judicial scrutiny involved the designation of property into two classifications, i.e., "exclusive" or ownership for personal purposes, and "non-exclusive" or ownership of public and private property used in public ways. The essential difference was that "exclusive" ownership carried with it the customary, community-shared expectation of privacy associated with the place, while "non-exclusive" ownership simply did not expect privacy. "Exclusive property" would encompass one's home, a reserved hotel room, an enclosed stall in a restroom, or one's body, as the latter is illustrated by Planned Parenthood of Central Missouri v. Danforth (428 US 52, 1976), where the U.S. Supreme Court invalidated several provisions of a Missouri statute that required an unmarried woman under eighteen years of age to have her parents' consent to an abortion and a married woman to have her husband's consent to an abortion. The court recognized the exclusiveness of a woman's property right in her own body, although the court was aware of "the deep and proper concern and interest that a devoted and unprotective husband has in his wife's pregnancy and in the growth and development of the fetus she is carrying." But in balancing the interests of all parties, the court found that the balance weighs in the woman's favor "inasmuch as it is the woman who physically bears the child and who is more directly and immediately affected by the pregnancy." The very next year the court in Carey v. Population Services International (431 US 678, 1977) determined that a "decision whether or not to beget or bear children is at the very heart" of the constitutionally protected right of privacy. Accordingly, the highest court struck down the New York statute that made it a crime for any person to sell or distribute contraceptives to minors, or for anyone other than a licensed pharmacist to distribute contraceptives to persons over sixteen years of age, or for anyone to advertise or display contraceptives. Although the court's holding was undoubtedly correct in a modern society, it should be observed that the court did not dwell upon property rights in protecting consensual sexual conduct. But in 1979 the same court, in Hollenbaugh v. Carnegie Free Library (439 US 1052), denied certiorari and in effect sanctioned the holding that the constitutional right of privacy did not encompass the adulterous relationship of two employees of a state-maintained library who were discharged after the female bore a child. Justice Thurgood Marshall wrote a stinging dissent contending that

> [s]uch administrative intermeddling with important personal rights merits more than minimal scrutiny. One such right, clearly implicated by petitioners' discharge, is that "of the individual . . . to engage in any of the common occupations of life" [citations omitted]. Perhaps even more vital is "the right to be free, except in very limited circumstances, from unwanted governmental intrusions into one's privacy" [citations omitted]. Although we never have demarcated the precise boundaries of this right, we have held that it broadly encompasses "freedom of personal choice in matters of marriage and family life" [citations omitted]. Petitioners' right to pursue an open rather than a clandestine personal relationship and to rear their child together in this environment closely resemble the other aspects of personal privacy to which we have extended constitutional protection.

It was not until the 1849 decision of Prince Albert v. Strange (41 Eng Rep 1171, aff. 64 Eng Rep 293) that in England the protection rested less on property right protection and more on breach of trust. The court enjoined the reproduction of several informal etchings which Prince Albert and Queen Victoria had made for their own amusement. The English court observed that "privacy is the right invaded."

Just a dozen years after the 1890 publication of 4 *Harvard Law Review* 193 the New York Court of Appeals in 1902 in Roberson v. Rochester Folding Box Company (64 NE 442) provided an illustration of the diversity of values inherent in the "right of privacy." Here a young woman whose photograph had been imprinted on flour advertisements without her permission was denied a cause of action for the invasion of her private interest. She was incensed by the use of her picture for commercial purposes and suffered mental distress. The New York court commented that "others would have appreciated the compliment to their beauty implied in the selection of her picture for such purposes; but, as it is distasteful to her, she seeks the aid of the Court." In a 4-3 decision the court refused to restrain the unauthorized use of the woman's portraiture on lithographic prints extensively used for advertising purposes; there simply was no legal right that had been infringed. Judge Gray, writing for the dissenters, found it inconceivable that there was no remedy under common law or in natural justice in keeping with "the progress of civilization . . . made possible as the result of new social or commercial conditions." This 1902 decision evoked much criticism from all quarters; the *New York Times* editorial of August 23, 1902, was so vehemently critical that a member of the majority of the New York Court of Appeals (Judge O'Brien) took the unprecedented step of writing an article in justification of the court's decision. See 2 *Columbia L Rev* 437 (1902).

The very next year the New York legislature enacted a statute (Laws 1903, c. 132, Sections 1 and 2) which permitted suit for the use of a person's "name, portrait or picture" for "advertising purposes" without that person's written permission or consent. From this humble beginning are derived Sections 50 and 51 of the New York Civil Rights Law, which will be delineated at length in §1.8 hereinafter. The first decision by an appellate court recognizing the right of privacy *without a statutory basis* was Pavesich v. New England Life Insurance Co. (50 SE 68), decided by the Georgia court in 1905. By recognizing the existence of a common law cause of action for invasion of privacy, the Georgia appellate court established an early pattern for recognition by the courts of other states of the right of privacy. Later, the Restatement of Torts, Section 867, entitled "Interference with Privacy," stated that "a person who reasonably and seriously interferes with another's interest in not having his affairs known to others or his likeness exhibited to the public is liable to the other." Indeed, the modern doctrine of the right of privacy is a development of the common law (with statutory assistance in several states) to fulfill a need for the protection of the interest which an individual has in living in modern society without unwarranted publicity.

1.2 THE RIGHT OF PRIVACY GENERALLY

Today the right of privacy is recognized in virtually all states either by statute or by common law decisions, except possibly in Rhode Island. See 58 *Neb L Rev* 808 (1980). The wide range of its coverage is evident in the fact that the

U.S. Supreme Court on November 17, 1985, refused to force a criminal suspect in an armed robbery case to undergo surgery so that the prosecutors could remove a bullet lodged under his collarbone and use the slug as evidence against him; in denying the request, the court ruled 9-0 that Mr. Lee's "interests in privacy and security," if breached, would constitute unreasonable search and seizure in violation of the Fourth Amendment! In 1978 the federal district court in New York in Forts v. Ward (471 F Supp 1095) demonstrated also the depth of judicial feeling on the general subject of privacy; here the right of privacy clashed with both the interests of the state of New York in prison administration and employment rights of prison workers. The issue involved assignments of male correction officers to jobs that permitted them to observe female inmates in the nude. Protection of the right of privacy of the female inmates was ordered by the trial court by the use of mottled or smoky glass to allow the male guards to make certain that someone was in the shower without being able to recognize the specific person. The court deemed the shining of flashlights into the cells to make certain that prisoners were in place to be a "violation of the inmate's right of privacy" because the inmates might at that very moment be using the toilet or sleeping with their bodies revealed. The court opined:

> While some out-of-the-ordinary steps are justifiable to reconcile the conflicting rights here, to require of an inmate extensive artificial procedures to preserve minimal human dignity in order to enable a man to be her guard at such times is, in my opinion, too high a price to pay for the equality of job opportunity achieved at its expense.

The Second U.S. Court of Appeals (621 F2d 1210, 1980), while vacating and remanding the case, nevertheless accepted the existence of a right of privacy for the prisoners.

Ralph Nader, author and lecturer on automotive safety, sued General Motors Corporation, charging defendants, inter alia, with an invasion of his right of privacy, in that General Motors allegedly conducted a campaign of intimidation against him in order to "suppress plaintiff's criticism of and prevent his disclosure of information" about General Motors automobiles. Specifically, Nader alleged that General Motors "(1) conducted a series of interviews with acquaintances of the plaintiff's questioning them and casting aspersions upon his political, social . . . racial and religious views, . . . his integrity, his sexual proclivities and inclinations and his personal habits; (2) kept him under surveillance in public places for an unreasonable length of time; (3) caused him to be accosted by girls for the purpose of entrapping him into illicit relationships; (4) made threatening, harassing and obnoxious telephone calls to him; (5) tapped his telephone and eavesdropped by means of mechanical and electronic equipment on his private conversation; and (6) conducted a continuing and harassing investigation of him." In Nader v. General Motors Corp. (255 NE2d 765, 1970) the New York Court of Appeals, interpreting the law of the District of

Columbia, found that only the allegations concerning excessive surveillance and tapping of the telephone (items 2 and 5 above) constituted "intrusions for the purpose of gathering information of a private and confidential nature," and, therefore, if true, were the only invasions of Nader's privacy. Subsequently, in August 1970, General Motors settled the case by payment of $425,000 (*New York Times*, August 14, 1970). It should be noted that "intrusion" had not been recognized as a tort in the District of Columbia as it had by the New Hampshire Supreme Court in Hamberger v. Eastman (206 A2d 239):

> We approve the extension of the tort of invasion of privacy to instances of intrusion, whether by physical trespass or not, into spheres from which an orindary man in a plaintiff's position could reasonably expect that the particular defendant should be excluded. Just as the Fourth Amendment has expanded to protect citizens from government intrusions where intrusion is not reasonably expected, so should tort law protect citizens from other citizens. The protection should not turn exclusively on the question of whether the intrusion involves a technical trespass under the law of property. The common law, like the Fourth Amendment, should "protect people, not places" [footnotes omitted].

It should also be observed that the right to privacy does not always refer to that which is not known to the public or is confidential. Indeed, the statutory right of privacy, as in New York, and perhaps the most traditional right of privacy in the sense of the common law, relates to the commercialization of one's face or name as under Sections 50 and 51 of the New York Civil Rights Law, delineated at §1.8 herein.

An interesting twist involving the right of privacy occurred in the California decision of Lasher v. Kleinberg (164 Cal Rptr 618, 1980). Here a mother, the minor child, and the child's guardian under law brought a paternity suit against the father, who admitted the paternity but filed a cross-complaint for fraud, negligent misrepresentation, and negligence. The father argued that the mother had falsely represented that she was taking birth control pills and that he had relied upon such representation in engaging in sexual intercourse with her. The father also claimed "mental agony and distress" plus the cost of support for the unwanted child. The trial court dismissed the cross-complaint, and the appellate court affirmed on the basis of the mother's "right of privacy," to wit: the claim presented by the father arose from conduct so intensely private that a court should not be asked to or attempt to resolve the claim. If the court were to supervise the promises made between two consenting adults as to the circumstances of their private and intimate sexual conduct, it would encourage unwarranted governmental intrusion into matters that affected an "individual right of privacy." With tongue in cheek, the court opined that there appeared no good reason why the father himself could not have taken contraceptive measures (which conclusion was a per se inquiry into the "right of privacy").

The complexity of the problem of recognizing the right of privacy is evident in two decisions of the Alaska Supreme Court: State v. Ravin (537 P2d 498,

1972) and State v. Erickson (574 P2d 1, 1978). The Ravin case dealt with the possession of marijuana in the home, and the Erickson case dealt with the possession of cocaine in the home. In the Ravin case the court protected the possessor's right of privacy in his home; marijuana, it pointed out, is the only controlled substance that can legally be possessed in the home without a prescription. On the other hand, in the Erickson case the court held that possession of cocaine in the home for personal use was not protected by the privacy defense. The distinction was apparently based on the nature of the relative effects of marijuana and cocaine on users of the drugs. Employing extensive scientific and sociological data, the Alaskan court concluded that the use of cocaine, even in small amounts in the home, presented a greater danger of harm to society than marijuana use in the home. What is most intriguing is the fact that both cases recognized that the home is the only place in which the fundamental right of privacy is recognized. But, as stated in the Erickson case, that fundamental right of privacy ''must yield when it interferes in a serious manner with the health, safety, rights and privileges of others or with the public welfare.''

1.3 TORTIOUS BASE FOR PROTECTION OF PERSONALITY

In 1966 Professor Harry Kalven, Jr., in an iconoclastic article entitled ''Privacy in Tort Law—Were Warren and Brandeis Wrong?'' (31 *Law and Contmp Prob* 327), questioned the desirability of protecting privacy through tort law, and concluded that, except for ''appropriations,'' the attempt to protect privacy through tort law is a mistake. Professor Kalven wrote that there has not been

> much interest displayed in what the underlying basis of liability is, although this has been the standard topic of analysis for all other tort categories. Does it matter whether the defendant knew the disclosure would be offensive, or whether he meant to refer to plaintiff at all, or whether he thought he was privileged by the public interest in the item? We are concerned, it must be emphasized, with a mass media tort where malicious intention is not likely to appear. The fact that we have no intelligible version of a prima facie case is only half the difficulty; the other half is that since Warren and Brandeis wrote, it has been agreed that there is a generous privilege to serve the public interest in news. And today, since New York Times Co. v. Sullivan (376 US 254, 1964), the privilege may arguably have some constitutional status. What is at issue, it seems to me, is whether the claim of privilege is not so overpowering as virtually to swallow the tort. What can be left of the vaunted new right after the claims of privilege have been confronted? . . . The lack of legal profile and the enormity of the counter-privilege converge to raise for me the question of whether privacy is really a viable tort remedy. The mountain, I suggest, has brought forth a pretty small mouse. . . .

The error in Professor Kalven's thinking, it is submitted, is evident from the fact that the tortious nature of the right of privacy has been widely accepted by the courts of all states. Professor Roscoe Pound, in his 1915 article ''Interests of Personality'' (28 *Harv L Rev* 343), echoed the tortious base for protection of personalilty:

[W]hen the individual interest is recognized, it is regarded at first as an interest in one's honor, in one's standing among brave men regardful of their honor, rather than as an interest in the integrity of the physical person. In Greek law every infringement of the personality of another is [hubris] (contumelia); the injury to honor, the insult, being the essential point, not the injury to the body. In Roman law, injury to the person is called iniuria, meaning originally insult, but coming to mean any willful disregard of another's personality. In consequence the beginnings of law measure composition not by the extent of the injury to the body, but by the extent of the injury to honor and the extent of the desire for vengeance thus aroused, since the interest secured is really the social interest in preserving the peace. . . .

. . . the law secures the interest of the individual in his honor at least as soon as his interest in his physical person, when presently it distinguishes between injuries to the person and injuries to honor or reputations.

But Professor Kalven responded about the ''relationship of privacy to autonomy or freedom'' as follows:

Do we value privacy only because it is useful to the strategy of protecting personal freedom or do we value it for its own sake independently of the practical consequences that intrusions into privacy may entail? Does privacy, absent a concern with freedom, reduce to a trivial quaint grievance? My deep personal hunch is that the topic is really freedom and that calling it privacy tends to obscure matters. In Griswold v. Connecticut (381 US 479, 1965), for example, is the grievance really the one the Supreme Court selected, namely, the predicted intrusions by police into the bedroom in the effort to enforce the law? Or is the grievance the law's effort to limit man's freedom to decide whether and when he will breed children? (23 *Rec NYC BA* 185, 1968)

Professor Louis Henkin, however, holds that the overriding accent on the freedom of choice is at the heart of the protection of privacy:

It has been insufficiently noticed that what the Court has been talking about is not at all what most people mean by privacy. None of the recent cases, and none of the older cases the Court cited (except those dealing with search and seizure under the Fourth Amendment), which the Justices have now swept together into the basket labeled ''right of privacy,'' deals with any of the matters that are the subject of the now-massive literature on privacy. . . . Primarily and principally the new Right of Privacy is a zone of prima facie autonomy, of presumptive immunity from regulation, in addition to that established by the First Amendment. The zone, Justice Blackman told us, consists of ''personal rights'' that can be deemed ''fundamental,'' that are ''implicit in the concept of ordered liberty.'' The right has ''some extension'' to marriage, sexual relations, contraception, unwanted children, family relations and parental autonomy. But we will know which rights are and which are not within the zone only case by case, with lines drawn and redrawn, in response to individual and societal initiatives and the imaginativeness of lawyers. (74 *Columbia L Rev* 1410)

1.4 PRIVACY PROTECTION IN THE COMPUTER AGE

The rapid advances in computer and telecommunications technology have taken individual records and individual papers from the home and private safes and out of the control of the individual. The recordkeeping explosion of the computer age has prompted both government and the private sector to keep previously unimagined records and papers relating to the individual. This boom in recordkeeping is traceable to at least three sociological factors which have given birth to the personal data services industry, to wit: (1) the tremendous expansion in the use of credit, credit cards, and even time-sharing arrangements; (2) the unparalleled mobility of population not only within the United States but throughout the world; and (3) the enormous increase in the size and quality of the work force.

The Privacy Act (1974), or PA (54 USC 522a), established the Privacy Protection Study Commission, which in 1977 found "imbalance in the relationship between individuals and recordkeeping organizations," and recommended three objectives to ensure effective and meaningful privacy protection for the individual: (1) minimize intrusiveness by balancing what an individual is expected to divulge and what he or she seeks in return; (2) maximize fairness by delineating the nature and the extent of recordkeeping operations; and (3) create legitimate and enforceable expectations of confidentiality by law or statute and by reasonable enforcement procedures. In addition, there are certain basic legal principles designed to protect individual privacy and individual liberties in any democratic society. First, an individual is entitled by law to have access to personal information held about him or her, particularly in computerized data banks. An individual is also entitled to control, in a reasonable manner, that information which is collected and disseminated about him or her. Second, to guarantee this right to individual privacy, the following must be provided for, either by statutes or laws: a statute of limitations or time period governing the initial collection of personal information; a delineation of the purposes for which such personal information may be used, clearly stated at the time of the initial collection of data; accurate, complete, and up-to-date information to ensure the quality of personal data; and rules prohibiting the disclosure of personal data.

To understand better this issue of "privacy protection," the Privacy Protection Study Commission identified five societal values that must be considered: (1) First Amendment interests; (2) freedom of information interests; (3) law enforcement; (4) costs; and (5) the federal-state relationship. Obviously, any restriction on the free flow of truthful information raises serious questions in a democratic society, but the individual must be given the right under specified conditions to exercise control over information about him or her, as, for example, by preventing a firm from mailing material to him or her that he or she regards as obscene (Lamont v. Postmaster General, 381 US 301, 1965). The Commission in its 1977 report entitled "Personal Privacy in an Information Society" stressed that "an individual has no constitutional protections against governmental demands for access to records that third parties maintained against him,'' but the Commission believed that individuals should have an assertable interest in records maintained about themselves by business, and recommended a federal statutory right of privacy.

In the field of insurance, the Privacy Protection Study Commission in its 1977 report wrote: ''The insurance industry is highly dependent upon recorded information about individuals. This dependence creates a number of privacy protection problems, some of which are inherent in the insurance system but can be controlled, and some of which present real or potential abuses that need to be eliminated'' (at p. 173). In Dunn v. Midwestern Indemnity Fire & Casualty Co. (472 F Supp 1106, Ohio 1979) the plaintiffs sought access to computer capabilities of five insurance companies including information about the computer equipment, raw data, programs, and data management systems. Plaintiffs had instituted a civil suit challenging the ''red-lining'' practices of these five insurers, which allegedly prevented the plaintiffs, a black or Negro couple, from procuring homeowner's insurance coverage on their residence, in violation of Title VIII of the Civil Rights Act (1968). The federal district court in Ohio found that racial discrimination was built into the computer system, and accordingly the discovery requests of the plaintiffs were deemed relevant and proper under Rule 26 (b) of the Federal Rules of Civil Procedure. Accordingly, plaintiffs' right of privacy was protected by the disclosure of the data to them, the very individuals for whom the personal data had been maintained.

It should readily be observed that this right of privacy is not absolute in an organized society, for privacy must always be balanced against other needs of society. For example, although a patient's legitimate expectation of privacy in medical records needs protection, it is equally clear that many legitimate uses are made of individually identifiable patient information. These uses would be impeded or made impossible by the creation of any absolute privacy right residing in the patient. These important uses include medical records; public health emergencies, such as the isolation of carriers of Legionnaire's Disease and other communicable diseases; audits of institutions which receive Medicare, Medicaid, and other federal or state health subsidies; review by insurance companies and other third-party payors of medical bills to determine eligibility and to process claims; investigations by welfare and other social service agencies in order to provide services; analyses by professional accrediting agencies and review boards to evaluate the quality of services; and the lawful obtaining of evidence by law enforcement agencies. Thus, the public's right to know is superior to the individual's right of privacy in most democratic societies. (See 13 *Texas Tech Law Review* 1361, 1982.)

1.5 THE RIGHT OF PRIVACY IN ABSENCE OF STATUTE

In a majority of jurisdictions today the right of privacy is recognized for its common law development absent a statute, except for statutes in Nebraska (Neb

Rev Stat Secs. 20-211 to 20-211, and 25-804.01), New York (see §1.8), Oklahoma (Okla Stat Ann, Title 21, Secs. 839.1 to 839.3), Utah (Utah Code Ann Secs. 76-9-401 to 76-9-406), Virginia (VA Code Secs. 2.1-377 to 2.1-386), and Wisconsin (Wis Stat Ann Sec. 895.50). In Indiana (Voelker v. Tyndall, 75 NE2d 548, 1947) the right of privacy was deemed to have derived from natural law and was guaranteed by federal and state constitutions so that between man and man (or woman and woman, or inter alia) the right of privacy must be respected. In New Jersey (McGovern v. Van Riper, 43 A2d 514, 1945) the right of privacy was described as "immutable and absolute, transcends the power of any authority to change or abolish it." And in Harris v. United States (331 US 145, 1947) the U.S. Supreme Court declared that "the rights of privacy . . . are to be regarded as of the very essence of constitutional liberty; and the guarantee of them is as important and as imperative as are the guarantees of the fundamental rights of the individual citizen."

Eavesdropping is one activity that has generally been held to be an invasion of privacy even in the absence of statute. In Dietemann v. Time, Inc. (449 F2d 245, 9th Cir, 1971) the defendant magazine was investigating medical quackery, and the plaintiff, according to the facts found by the trial judge, was indeed a prime example of a quack. Two reporters from the magazine entered plaintiff's home, one of whom represented that he desired treatment. During the course of the treatment the other reporter photographed, without the knowledge of the plaintiff, the very premises and transmitted conversations by a hidden microphone to a tape recorder in an automobile parked nearby. In affirming judgment for the plaintiff, the Ninth U.S. Court of Appeals observed:

> Plaintiff's den was a sphere from which he could reasonably expect to exclude eavesdropping newsmen. He invited two of defendant's employees to the den. One who invites another to his home or office takes a risk that the visitor may not be what he seems, and that the visitor may repeat all he hears and observes when he leaves. But he does not and should not be required to take the risk that what is heard and seen will be transmitted by photograph or recording, or in our modern world, in full living color and hi-fi to the public at large or to any segment of it that the visitor may select. A different rule could have a most pernicious effect upon the dignity of man and it would surely lead to guarded conversations and conduct where candor is most valued, e.g. in the case of doctors and lawyers.

On the other hand, in Pearson v. Dodd (410 F2d 701, DC Cir 1969; cert den 395 US 947, 1969), the District of Columbia Court of Appeals refused to impose liability on the recipients of stolen papers for an invasion of plaintiff's right of privacy:

> Although appellee's complaint charges that appellants aided and abetted in the removal of the documents, the undisputed facts, narrowed by the District Judge with the concurrence of counsel, established only that appellants received copies of the documents knowing that they had been removed without authorization. If we were to hold appel-

lants liable for invasion of privacy on these facts, we would establish the proposition that one who receives information from an intruder, knowing it has been obtained by improper intrusion, is guilty of a tort. A person approached by an eavesdropper with an offer to share in the information gathered through the eavesdropping would perhaps play the nobler part should he spurn the offer and shut his ears. However, it seems to us that at this point it would place too great a strain on human weakness to hold one liable in damages who merely succumbs to temptation and listens.

It should be noted that eavesdropping or surveillance reasonably carried out for legitimate purposes is not an invasion of the right of privacy, as illustrated by a credit reporting agency gathering information (Tureen v. Equifax, Inc., 571 F2d 411, 8th Cir 1978) or by an investigation of a workers' compensation claim (McLain v. Boise Cascade Corp., 533 P2d 343, Ore 1975).

1.6 STATUTORY BASIS FOR RIGHT OF PRIVACY

As disclosed in §1.5 herein, there are at least six states that rest their action for invasion of the right of privacy upon statutes. Both Nebraska (Brunson v. Ranks Army Store, 73 NW2d 803, 1955) and Wisconsin (Yoeckel v. Samonig, 75 NW2d 925, 1956), for example, have flatly declared that there was no common law right of action for invasion of privacy. The state of Connecticut, on the other hand, in Korn v. Rennison (156 A2d 476, 1959) opined that "the common law is not static and its protecting arm does not become immobilized from lack of precedent." (Connecticut is a non-statutory state.)

In addition to state legislative enactments, there are federal statutes that in recent years have endeavored to spell out the reasonable bounds for protection of individual privacy, to wit: the Fair Credit Reporting Act (1970), or FCRA (15 USC 1681-1681t); the Privacy Act (1974), or PA (5 USC 522a); the Right to Financial Privacy Act (1978), or RFPA (12 USC 3401-3422); the Privacy Protection Act (1980), or PPA (42 USC 2000aa-11); the Electronic Fund Transfer Act (1980), or EFTA (15 USC 1693); the Family Education Rights and Privacy Act (1974), or FERPA (20 USC 1221); and the Crime Control Act (1973), or CCA (42 USC 3789g), for example. FCRA was perhaps the first federal legislative assault upon private informational activities that violate privacy; the Act mandated reasonable procedures by credit reporting agencies to provide credit information in a fair and equitable manner and with full regard for "the confidentiality, accuracy, relevancy, and proper utilization of the information." Under Section 1681 (a) (4) of FCRA emphasis is placed upon "respect for the consumer's right to privacy." Fortunately, however, consumer credit reports are deemed "commercial speech" outside of the protection of the First Amendment so that credit reporting activities can be carried out (Millstone v. O'Hanlon Reports, Inc., 528 F2d 829, 8th Cir 1976). It is the individual, not the business entity, that is given protection against invasion of privacy under FCRA. When adverse action is taken on an application for credit, insurance, or employment, for example, and the adverse report is based wholly or in part on information in a consumer report, FCRA requires that the user of the data advise the consumer of the adverse action and supply the name and address of the consumer reporting agency. (A "consumer reporting agency" is defined under Section 1681 a (f) as including an agency that acts for monetary fees, dues, or on a cooperative nonprofit basis and regularly engages in whole or in part in gathering or evaluating information on consumers in order to distribute such information to third parties engaged in commerce. See Porter v. Talbot Perkins Children's Services, 355 F Supp 174, SDNY 1973.) The thrust of FCRA was not to preclude dissemination of critical credit data but only to curb unreasonable or careless invasion of consumer privacy (In Re TRW, Inc., 460 F Supp 1007, ED Mich 1978). The user of the data does not violate FCRA if he uses the data before the consumer has had the opportunity to object to the accuracy or relevancy of the data.

FCRA was bitterly criticized by the federal district court in Minnesota in Henry v. Forbes (433 F Supp 5, 1976), which declared:

> The Act does not provide a private remedy for all illicit or abusive use of information about consumers. . . . individuals are not protected against the abuse of the credit reporting apparatus unless their circumstances are within the narrow bounds of coverage under the Act. . . . [The individual has] no remedy unless the information were used in violation of common law privacy rights (requiring highly public, outrageous conduct to make a cause of action).

FCRA does not totally preempt state common law privacy actions, according to Freeman v. Southern National Bank (531 F Supp 94, SD Tex 1982): "actions at common law are not preempted if false information is conveyed with willful intent to injure the consumer" (15 USC 1681h (e)). In Hood v. Dun & Bradstreet, Inc. (486 F2d 25, 5th Cir 1973) the court pointed out that FCRA "does not preclude an action at common law except where information that would give rise to a cause of action is obtained by the complainant pursuant to the provisions of the Act."

RFPA limits the federal government's access to individual records held by banks and financial institutions, for unwarranted intrusion by government into an individual's financial affairs is barred. But a bank or financial institution is protected from liability under RFPA if it acts in good faith (12 USC 3417 (a)). Section 3402 of RFPA provides that no federal governmental authority may have access to information in the financial records of a "customer" of a bank or financial institution, except through one of five disclosure mechanisms: (1) customer authorization; (2) search warrant; (3) administrative subpoena; (4) judicial subpoena; or (5) formal written request, including notice to the customer so that a customer might have the opportunity to challenge the governmental request for data. Unfortunately, under Section 3413 (g) of RFPA the government may almost freely seek "name, address, account number and type of account." Interestingly, RFPA was the Congressional response to United States

v. Miller (425 US 435, 1975), wherein the U.S. Supreme Court had held that the individual did not have privacy expectations concerning his bank records. Legislative history shows that RFPA was passed simply to overturn that wrong decision. (See HR Rep. No. 1383, 95th Cong, 2d Sess, 1978.)

PPA establishes the procedures for law enforcement agencies to acquire print media records, but it accords special protection against searches and seizures of materials in the possession of the media and their representatives by federal, state, and local law enforcement agencies. Such materials are subject to seizure by law enforcement agencies *only* if the custodian of the materials is suspected of criminal activity or to prevent death, serious bodily injury, or destruction of evidence. Reporters and other protected persons who believe their right of privacy has been violated may sue for damages, the minimum award being $1,000. Interestingly, the U.S. Supreme Court decision in Zurcher v. Stanford Daily (436 US 547, 1978), which delineated articles and photographs of a clash between demonstrators and police at a hospital that were published by a student newspaper, prompted the enactment of PPA, for that decision permitted law enforcement officials to have access to the student newspaper's files.

EFTA requires each bank to notify its customers about routine third-party disclosures of personal records.

FERPA is popularly known as the Buckley Amendment and requires schools and colleges to give students or their parents certain rights to personal information, but sharply limits disclosure of such personal information to third parties. See Girardier v. Webster College (563 F2d 1267, 8th Cir 1977).

CCA mandates that states that received federal funds for upgrading their criminal justice information systems adopt privacy and security programs to protect and regulate information in those systems.

Another piece of federal regulation is the Omnibus Crime Control and Safe Streets Acts (1968) or OCCSSA (18 2510-2520), which deals with privacy matters in the willful interception of any wire or oral communication.

But the prime federal legislation is the Privacy Act (1974), which is intended to "provide certain safeguards for an individual against an invasion of personal privacy" by requiring federal agencies to observe certain requirements and prohibitions regarding the maintenance of personal information. The operative provisions of PA are contained in the Freedom of Information Act (1966), delineated herein at §1.7; FOIA prohibits agencies from disclosing records pertaining to an individual without his or her consent except under prescribed circumstances. PA, while directed to the public sector, governs the collection, maintenance, use, and disclosure of federal governmental records on individuals. Only "relevant and necessary" data may be gathered by the federal government; in Wolman v. United States (501 F Supp, DC 1980) the court held that the Selective Service System's requirement that draft registrants supply Social Security numbers violated Section 7 of PA; it was pointed out that one of the purposes of Section 7 of PA was to block any further expansion of the use of Social Security numbers as a universal identifier. The individual under PA may gain access to his records kept by government, and the governmental agencies are required to disclose annually what records they keep and afford individuals a limited right of access to an opportunity to correct agency records. It is a misdemeanor for a government employee to knowingly and willfully make an unauthorized disclosure of a person's records or to maintain records that do not meet the requirement of annual notice. (See 5 USC 552 (i) (1).) But among the exceptions to the prohibition against nonconsensual agency disclosure of personal records is disclosure for a "routine use" (5 USC 552a (a)), which is defined as "the use of such record for a purpose which is compatible with the purpose for which it was collected." The only restraint on the federal agency's utilization of the "routine use" provision is the requirement that the agency publish information about its "routine uses," that the agency enable interested persons to comment on any new intended uses of such records, and that the agency inform sources of information of the "routine uses" to which the information may be put. The "routine use" exception is only one of the twelve exceptions to PA's prohibition against disclosure of an individual's personal record without that individual's consent. The other exceptions pertain to other agency employees with a "need to know" clearance; to others as required under FOIA; to the Census Bureau, for use solely as a statistical record; to the National Archives; to a law enforcement agency upon written request of the agency head; to Congress, for compelling health or safety reasons; to the Comptroller General, pursuant to a court order; or to a consumer reporting agency pursuant to the Debt Collection Act. (See 5 USC 552a (b) (2) to (12).)

The Privacy Act (1974) or PA contains both criminal and civil remedies for violations of its provisions, but they are generally ineffective since there is no meaningful relief to an individual for agency violations of PA. In a civil relief the individual's damages are difficult to measure; furthermore, the agency action must have been intentional or willful and have had a profound adverse effect upon the plaintiff individual. See Fitzpatrick v. Internal Revenue Service (665 F2d 237, 11th Cir, 1982). Injunctive relief is available only to obtain access to records or to amend records, not to enjoin the agency from disclosure (Edison v. Department of the Army, 672 F2d 840, 11th Cir, 1982).

PA is heavily weighed down with both general exemptions (such as permitting the Central Intelligence Agency [CIA] and criminal law enforcement agencies to exempt their systems of records) and with specific exemptions which apply to classified information, law enforcement investigatory information, records maintained in connection with providing protection to the President, statistical records, military service records, government contracts or access to classified data, federal employment testing records, material used to determine promotions in the armed services, etc.

PA has been amended three times from 1974 to 1986: in 1982 a new exception was added to the disclosure prohibitions made to consumer credit reporting agencies pursuant to the Debt Collection Act (1982) or DCA (5 USC 552a (b) (12)). A 1984 amendment solved many of the interrelationships with FOIA.

See 5 USC 552a (q) (2), when Congress passed the Central Intelligence Agency Information Act (1984) or CIAIA (50 USC 401), which added a provision to PA prohibiting an agency from relying on an exception in PA to withhold records from an individual that would otherwise be accessible under FOIA.

The *New York Times* (January 18, 1986, at p. 50) reported a decision by the U.S. Court of Appeals for the District of Columbia which construed the Privacy Act as mandating a clear-cut decision in a disputed security case. It seems that the unidentified woman applied in 1980 for a job with the U.S. State Department, and in a routine investigation, inconsistencies were discovered between the information she provided and the information she had previously furnished to the Veterans Administration. In 1981 she was appointed to a high-level job in another federal agency that required security clearance, and she had trouble obtaining the clearance due to the inconsistencies in her personnel record. She challenged the information in the State Department file and asked for a review, but the State Department "simply threw up its hands, said it could not resolve the conflict between the agent's and Jane Doe's stories and put everything in the record." The federal district court ruled that her records were "as accurate as is reasonably necessary," but the appellate court reversed, declaring that the State Department must avoid "McCarthyesque innuendo" and must decide the truth about the dispute, rather than simply presenting both sides of the case in its records. The appellate court said that the Privacy Act imposed a substantial duty on each federal agency "to maintain its records with accuracy and to avoid harming individuals by keeping sloppy or willfully inaccurate records . . . [and that duty] cannot be discharged by the maintenance of conflicting reports and the lament that it would be too difficult to determine the truth." In short, the Privacy Act mandated "such accuracy as is reasonably necessary to assure fairness to the individual." The Debt Collection Act was designed to facilitate the collection of debts owed to the United States by permitting the utilization of a number of debt collection techniques including governmental use of *private* debt collection agencies. Federal agencies are therefore authorized to disclose information regarding debts to such private agencies, subject to PA. But the bottom line is that the federal agency need not obtain the consent of the individual before disclosing the individual's records to a consumer reporting agency that is in the business of collecting and evaluating consumer credit information for transmission to third parties. DCA also permits the Internal Revenue Service to disclose to other agencies the mailing address of a taxpayer for purposes of locating him and seeking to collect a debt (26 USC 6103 (m) (2)). Indeed, DCA represents the first significant statutory inroad on the protections of PA.

1.7 FREEDOM OF INFORMATION ACT

Of all federal legislation, probably few federal enactments have the same close relationship to the right of privacy as the Freedom of Information Act

(1966) or FOIA (5 USC 552), which in effect gives every citizen the right to look at government records; thereupon this right may infringe upon the privacy rights of other persons. At the same time, FOIA poses problems which can violate the right of privacy, as where private litigants successfully obtain information about their individual business competitors or litigation adversaries. The legislative purpose behind FOIA is to compel each federal agency to make ''promptly available to any person'' records that he has identified and requested in accordance with procedures amplified in the agency's rules. The obligation ''promptly'' to disclose is general and enforceable in federal district courts in a proceeding given precedence on the court's calendar and tried de novo with the burden of proof upon the agency to sustain its action. The ''right to know'' doctrine generally prevails on behalf of the public, and by the 1974 amendment federal agencies were given ten working days to respond to a request for identification of documents and to decide whether to release or withhold the requested information. (This period of time may be extended for an additional ten days by written notice but only if the request is voluminous or requires assistance from the field.) A denial of information permits the requester to appeal to the ''head of the agency,'' who must respond in twenty days; the next step is action in federal district court if the matter is unresolved. Where the federal agency refuses the request for information on the basis that litigation with the agency is or will shortly be on the way, a few courts have agreed with the agency's refusal, as in Fruehauf Corp. v. Thornton (507 F2d 1253, 6th Cir 1974) and Renegotiation Board v. Bannercraft Clothing Co. (415 US 1, 1974). The U.S. Supreme Court set forth some guidelines as to the appropriate effect of a litigant's use of FOIA as a discovery tool in National Labor Relations Board (NLRB) v. Sears, Roebuck & Co. (421 US 132, 1975). However, discovery under the Federal Rules of Civil Procedure (where the federal government is a party to the proceedings) is the more appropriate method of obtaining documents for use in all types of legal proceedings. Under Rules 26 (b) and (c), if documents are ''relevant to the subject matter involved in the pending action,'' the documents are presumptively disclosable; the fact that a document falls within an FOIA exemption does not give an agency a reason not to provide the document in a discovery proceeding (Baldridge v. Shapiro, 455 US 345, 1982). But the FOIA request for documents can be made by any person without showing need or relevancy (Firestone Tire and Rubber Co. v. Coleman, 432 F Supp 1359, ND Ohio 1976), and there are no restrictions on the use of the documents, which means that frequently the privacy of individuals may not be protected. Government reports can fall within the exception to the hearsay rule as set forth in Rule 803 (8) (c) of the Federal Rules of Evidence (Robbins v. Whelan, 653 F2d 47, 1st Cir 1981). Government records are admissible under the Business Records Act (28 USC 1732).

Unfortunately, unfair disclosure of personal data has become a problem, such as disclosure of statements by sworn witnesses taken by government in investigation of unfair labor practices (Temple-Eastex, Inc. v. NLRB, 410 F Supp 183, ED Tex 1976); disclosure of individual offers in compromise actually accepted by the Internal Revenue Service (Robins & Weill, Inc. v. U.S., 63 FRD 73, MDNC 1974); or disclosure of a government investigatory accident report based upon hearsay evidence (Moore-McCormack Lines, Inc. v. ITO Corp., 508 F2d 945, 4th Cir 1974). On the other hand, there are nine exceptions or exemptions which permit the federal government to withhold informational data, to wit: (1) documents classified by executive order concerning national defense or foreign policy; (2) internal personnel rules and practices of a government agency; (3) documents exempt under other federal statutes, such as income tax returns and patent applications; (4) trade secrets and commercial and financial information obtained and classified as privileged or confidential; (5) interagency or intra-agency memoranda or letters; (6) individual personnel and medical files; (7) investigatory records compiled for law enforcement purposes; (8) reports of agencies responsible for regulation or supervision of financial institutions; and (9) geological and geophysical data, such as the location of oil wells (5 USC 552 (b)). Exemption 6 poses a grave threat to the right of privacy, for these personnel and medical files are the records that concern the private lives of individuals. Although in theory there is a stated exemption, actual practice has resulted in disclosures that have caused irreparable harm to individuals. Some courts have permitted disclosure of personnel and medical files by simply balancing the interests between the public's right to know and the individual's right to privacy (Common Cause, Inc. v. Ruff, 467 F Supp 941, DC 1979). Actually, it is the clear-cut policy of most government agencies to disclose exempt materials unless there is a compelling reason not to do so. These disclosures constitute unwarranted invasions of personal privacy and should be closely monitored. Incidentally, individuals who have supplied information to the government and who object to the release of that information to other parties have no greater rights than the parties requesting that information. See Chrysler Corp. v. Brown (441 US 281, 1979).

In NLRB v. Sears, Roebuck & Co. (421 US 132, 1975) the U.S. Supreme Court was concerned about Exemption 5 on interagency or intra-agency memoranda or letters. Justice Byron R. White took occasion to opine:

> The parties are in apparent agreement that Exemption 5 withholds from a member of the public documents which a private party could not discover in litigation with the agency. EPA v. Mink (410 US 73, 85-86, 1973). Since virtually any document not privileged may be discovered by the appropriate litigant, it is relevant to his litigation; and since the Act clearly intended to give any member of the public as much right to disclosure as one with a special interest therein, it is reasonable to construe Exemption 5 to exempt those documents, and only those documents, normally privileged in the civil discovery context. The privileges claimed by the government to be relevant to this case are (i) the "generally . . . recognized" privilege for "confidential intra-agency advisory opinions, . . . " disclosure of which would be "injurious to the consultative

> functions of government. . . . " EPA v. Mink, supra, at 86-87 (sometimes referred to as "executive privilege"), and (ii) the attorney-client and attorney work product privileges generally available to all litigants.

The court recognized the federal government's executive privileges and ruled that the petitioner's request for "Advice and Appeals Memoranda" which "direct the filing of a complaint . . . fall[s] within the coverage of Exemption 5."

In Weber Aircraft Corp. v. U.S. (686 F2d 638, 9th Cir 1982; rev 104 S Ct 1488, 1984) the principal issue was whether witness statements given under a promise of confidentiality to an Air Force investigation board are exempt from the mandatory disclosure provisions of FOIA. Here a Captain Hoover had sustained serious injuries when he ejected from an Air Force plane after the engine had failed. The Air Force conducted a "collateral investigation" to "preserve available evidence for use in claims and litigation" and a "safety investigation" which produced a Mishap Report which the Air Force labeled a "privileged document" for the purpose of accident prevention. When Captain Hoover sued Weber Aircraft and Mills Manufacturing Corporation, the designer and manufacturer of his parachute and harness assembly, these defendants requested copies of all Air Force investigation reports pertaining to the accident. The Air Force released to the defendants the complete record of the "collateral investigation" but withheld under Exemption 5 a number of documents including agency memoranda used in the deliberative process. The Ninth U.S. Circuit Court of Appeals ruled that the Air Force "may withhold any 'reasonable segregable' portion of the witnesses' statements containing advice, opinions, or recommendations . . . but must disclose any factual portion of the witnesses' statements at issue." The U.S. Supreme Court in 1984 reversed in part by holding that Exemption 5 does incorporate the "civil-discovery privilege for official government information," and therefore intra-agency memoranda or letters which would normally be protected from disclosure in civil litigation fall within Exemption 5, but factual material is still available.

Exemption 4 was discussed by the District of Columbia Circuit Court of Appeals in National Parks and Conservation Assn. v. Morton (498 F2d 765, 1974). Circuit Judge Tamm observed:

> In order to bring a matter (other than a trade secret) within (the fourth) exemption, it must be shown that the information is (a) commercial or financial, (b) obtained from a person, and (c) privileged or confidential. Since the parties agree that the matter in question is financial information obtained from a person and that it is not privileged, the only issue on appeal is whether the information is "confidential" within the meaning of the exemption. Unfortunately, the statute contains no definition of the word "confidential." In the past, our decisions concerning this exemption have [been] guided by the following passage from the Senate Report, . . .
>
> > "This exception is necessary to protect the confidentiality of information which is obtained by the Government through questionnaires or other inquiries but which

would customarily not be released to the public by the person from whom it was obtained. . . . ''

To summarize, commercial or financial matter is ''confidential'' for purposes of the exemption if disclosure of the information is likely to have either of the following effects: (1) to impair the Government's ability to obtain necessary information in the future, or (2) to cause substantial harm to the competitive position of the person from whom the information was obtained.

The court then concluded:

As we have already explained, however, Section 552 (b) (4) may . . . be invoked for the benefit of the person who has provided commercial or financial information if it can be shown that public disclosure is likely to cause substantial harm to his competitive position. Appellant argues that such a showing cannot be made in this case because the concessioners are monopolists, protected from competition during the term of their contracts and enjoying a statutory preference over other bidders at renewal time. In other words, appellant argues that disclosure cannot impair the concessioners' competitive position because they have no competition. While this argument is very compelling, we are reluctant to accept it without first providing appellee the opportunity to develop a fuller record in the district court. It might be shown, for example, that disclosure of information about concession activities will injure the concessioner's competitive position in a non-concession enterprise. In that case disclosure would be improper. This matter is therefore remanded to the district court for the purpose of determining whether public disclosure of the information in question poses the likelihood of substantial harm to the competitive positions of the parties from whom it has been obtained. . . .

Exemption 2 was the subject of Department of Air Force v. Rose (425 US 352, 1976) when respondents, student editors and former student editors of the *New York University Law Review* researching disciplinary systems and procedures at military service institutions for an article in the *Law Review*, were denied access to case summaries of honor and ethics hearings, although these summaries were posted on bulletin boards at the Air Force Academy. The basis for the government's rejection was Exemption 2, relating ''solely to the internal personnel rules and practices.'' Although the federal district court favored the government's position because the disclosures of those files ''would constitute a clearly unwarranted invasion of personal privacy,'' the Second U.S. Court of Appeals reversed, finding Exemption 2 inapplicable, and the U.S. Supreme Court affirmed by bringing to bear upon their opinion Exemption 6 as to individual personnel and medical files. The highest court opined that personnel files are not wholly excluded, and that the appellate court properly ordered the agency ''to produce the case summaries in the District Court for an 'in camera' examination to eliminate information that could result in identifying cadets involved in Honor or Ethics Code violations.''

What constitutes identifying information regarding a subject cadet must be weighed not only from the viewpoint of the public, but also from the vantage of those who would

> have been familiar, as fellow cadets or Academy staff, with other aspects of his career at the Academy . . . the risk to privacy interests of a former cadet, particularly one who has remained in the military, posed by his identification by otherwise unknowing former colleagues or instructors cannot be rejected as trivial.
>
> To be sure, redaction cannot eliminate all risks of identifiability, as any human approximation risks some degree of imperfection, and the consequences of exposure of identity can admittedly be severe. But redaction is a familiar technique in other contexts and exemptions to disclosure under the Act were intended to be practical workable concepts. Moreover, we repeat Exemption 6 does not protect against disclosure every incidental invasion of privacy—only such disclosures as constitute ''clearly unwarranted'' invasions of personal privacy.

The dissenting opinion of Chief Justice Warren Burger highlighted his view that the court

> blandly ignores and thereby frustrates the congressional intent by refusing to weigh, realistically, the grave consequences implicit in release of this particular information, in any form, against the relatively inconsequential claim of ''need'' for the material alleged in the complaint. . . . It is indeed difficult to attribute to Congress a willingness to subject an individual citizen to the risk of possible severe damage to his reputation simply to permit law students to invade individual privacy to prepare a law journal article. Its definition of a ''clearly unwarranted invasion of personal privacy'' as equated with ''protecting an individual's private affairs from unnecessary public scrutiny. . . . '' S. Rep. No. 813, at 9 (emphasis applied), would otherwise be rendered meaningless. Moreover, excision . . . would place an intolerable burden upon a district court . . . there is nothing in the legislative history of the original Act or its amendments which would require a district court to construct, in effect, a new document. Yet, the excision process mandated here could only require such a sweeping reconstruction of the material that the end product would constitute an entirely new document.

Exemption 7 protects ''investigatory records compiled for law enforcement purposes'' from disclosure that would ''constitute an unwarranted invasion of privacy.'' In Pratt v. Webster (508 F Supp 751, DC 1981) the petitioner filed an FOIA request with the Federal Bureau of Investigation (FBI) for materials in the FBI's possession relating to him, but he found most of the requested materials to contain deletions; the FBI had also withheld the names of FBI agents and clerical staff, the names of non-federal law enforcement personnel, as well as information regarding investigations by third parties. The court upheld the FBI, pointing out that since the FBI agent's interest in privacy is not as strong as that of the average private citizen, the court must take the steps to protect privacy. It would appear that the court was in error in withholding the names of publicly paid law enforcement personnel acting within the scope of their duties.

The federal government is not alone in opening official files to public view as under FOIA. Many states have statutory counterparts, and court decisions like City of St. Matthews v. Voice of St. Matthews (519 SW2d, Ky 1974) have given impetus to access to information held by public bodies; in this case the Kentucky Court of Appeals recognized the right of a newspaper to inspect tax assessment records, payroll records, building permits, and a wide variety of other public records, subject only to showing "a purpose which tends to advance or further a wholesome public interest or a legitimate private interest." The court spelled out the "rules" in these words:

(1) The inspection shall be conducted at reasonable times and places and in such a manner as not to unduly interfere with the proper operation of the office of the custodian of the records. (2) The records sought to be inspected are not exempt from inspection by law. (3) The disclosure of the information would not be detrimental to the public interest or violative of confidentiality under countervailing public policy entitled to greater weight than the policy favoring free access to public records.

1.8 NEW YORK LAW OF PRIVACY

The state of New York has been in the forefront of recognition of the right of privacy, particularly after the 1903 enactment of Sections 50 and 51 of the New York Civil Rights Law (which includes the 1921 amendment). This legislative enactment makes it both a misdemeanor and a tort to make use of the name, portrait, or picture of any person for advertising purposes or for purposes of trade without his written consent:

§50. *Right of privacy*
A person, firm or corporation that uses for advertising purposes, or for the purposes of trade, the name, portrait or picture of any living person without having first obtained the written consent of such person, or if a minor of his or her parent or guardian, is guilty of a misdemeanor.

§51. *Action for injunction and for damages*
Any person whose name, portrait or picture is used within this state for advertising purposes or for the purposes of trade without the written consent first obtained as above provided may maintain an equitable action in the supreme court of this state against the person, firm or corporation so using his name, portrait or picture, to prevent and restrain the use thereof; and may also sue and recover damages for any injuries sustained by reason of such use and if the defendant shall have knowingly used such person's name, portrait or picture in such manner as is forbidden or declared to be unlawful by the last section, the jury, in its discretion, may award exemplary damages. . . .

The statute may be briefly annotated as follows: "person, firm or corporation" includes even the state, as in Seidelman v. State of New York (110 NYS2d 380, Ct Cl, 1952); "use" means intent to capitalize upon, not an isolated or unintentional act (Ladany v. William Morrow & Co., 465 F Supp 870, SDNY 1978), although the "use" must occur within one year of the suit under Section 215 (3) of the Civil Practice Act; the use must be "within this state," which would include an out-of-state football game televised into New York (Gautier

v. Pro-Football, Inc., 107 NE2d 485, 1952); "for advertising purposes" has been construed to include any solicitation for patronage (Flores v. Mosler Safe Co., 164 NE2d 853, 1959), although solicitation incidental to news-gathering is not encompassed (Humiston v. Universal Film Mfg. Co., 178 NYS 752, 1919); "for purposes of trade" means for the benefit or gain of the defendant (Almind v. Sea Beach Railway Co., 141 NYS 842, 1913), but a tenant could not recover for her landlord's unauthorized entering and photographing plaintiff's apartment (Novel v. Beacon Operating Co., 446 NYS2d 118, 1982), and again news-gathering is not encompassed (Lerman v. Chuckleberry Publishing, Inc., 496 F Supp 1105, SDNY 1980); "name, portrait or picture" has been interpreted by the courts in literal words necessitating positive identification (Lawrence v. Ylla, 55 NYS2d 343, 1945); "any living person" emphasizes that the statute protects only live human beings, not corporations or partnerships (Dauer & Fittipaldi, Inc. v. Twenty-First Century Communications, Inc., 349 NYS2d 736, 1973), and no other person can enforce the right of privacy, for it is a personal right (Runyon v. U.S., 281 F2d 590, 5th Cir 1960); and "without having first obtained written consent" means exactly what it says (Wilk v. Andrea Radio Corp., 200 NYS2d 522, 1960). The statute was held constitutional in 1908 in Rhodes v. Sperry & Hutchinson Co. (85 NE 1097, NY), which was affirmed in 1911 by the U.S. Supreme Court (220 US 502).

Court decisions over the past years have given substance to the New York statute, as illustrated by Lahr v. Adell Chemical Co. (300 F2d 256, 1st Cir, 1962). Here plaintiff, a well-known stage, screen, and radio actor, brought suit against the manufacturer of the detergent "Lestoil," alleging, inter alia, invasion of his right of privacy by defendant's imitation of his distinctive voice and comic style delivery, which had made him widely known and readily recognizable. Defendant in a television commercial advertising its product had imitated plaintiff's voice and comic style delivery in a cartoon film of a duck advertising the product. Plaintiff contended that this use of his voice and comic style delivery was an appropriation of his creative talent as well as causing damage to his acting career by the seeming appearance that he had been reduced to giving anonymous television commercials. The court disagreed and ruled that his allegations did not state a cause of action under Sections 50 and 51 of the New York Civil Rights Law:

> Any right resulting from the special New York statute, sometimes called the right of privacy statute, flow[s] from the use, for commercial purposes of a party's "name, portrait, or picture. . . . " Plaintiff's claim here, at best, is that, though the picture was that of a duck, the voice was the "name" which he enlarges to "identity" of the plaintiff. The statute is very specific. If the Legislature intended that whenever an anonymous speaker extolled a commercial product a cause of action arose (and criminal penalties could be imposed) if anyone could claim the voice was mistaken as his, it should have used a phrase of more general import. In the absence of any New York authority "name" can be given no such catholic connotation.

In Youssoupoff v. Columbia Broadcasting System the plaintiff was a member of the former Russian royal family, and in 1916 he had admittedly murdered the Russian monk Rasputin; he had written two books in which he described the plot and the details of the killing of Rasputin, who had an evil influence on the Czarina and through her on the Czar. The defendant broadcast a dramatic sketch or play in which an actor impersonated the plaintiff, who thereupon sued for invasion of his privacy. But the New York Supreme Court, in New York County, in 1963 found no invasion of privacy:

> The privilege to use a person's name or photograph in portrayals of current news or past events of legitimate public or general interest does not . . . extend to "commercialization of . . . personality through a form of treatment distinct from the designation of news or information. . . . " The portrayal of the plaintiff by the actor who impersonated him in the broadcast . . . [did not] in any way injure in the slightest plaintiff's character or reputation.

In Creel v. Crown Publishers, Inc., the New York Appellate Division, First Department, on December 19, 1985, dismissed a complaint by the plaintiffs whose nude photograph appeared in a book, *World Guide to Nude Beaches and Recreation*. It seems that plaintiffs, while vacationing on the island of St. Maarten, met defendant's photographer, who took with their consent various photographs. The trial court granted summary judgment for the plaintiffs, finding that

> the publication of the photographs was for purposes of trade within the Civil Rights Law and rejected any claim that such pictures were "newsworthy." It saw the primary purpose of the book as one to print 200 pictures of totally exposed persons, and not the dissemination of any information. In Special Term's view, the photograph's use was designed to promote the commercial sales of the defendant's book, and hence violated the Civil Rights Law.

But the appellate court reversed, ruling that

> [a] guide to beaches where nude bathing is permitted is a matter of some public interest and the use of photographs with the text is protected by constitutional safeguards and is outside the protection of the Civil Rights Law. The focus of inquiry in applying the "public interest" exception is not only upon the particular photograph but also upon the article or book within which the photograph appears. Here, the photograph was utilized to illustrate a guide book which disseminated information concerning a matter of public interest and was not, therefore, utilized for purposes of "trade" within the meaning of the Civil Rights Law. That plaintiffs may deem the use of the photograph "offensive" cannot vitiate its use once the finding has been made that such use is outside the scope of sections 50 and 51. . . .

In Selsman v. Universal Photo Books, Inc., an infant plaintiff, an actress and model employed in the Walt Disney film *The Light in the Forest*, had, unknown to her, her photograph taken showing her focusing a Minox camera. The New York Supreme Court, New York County, in 1963, declared that the subsequent use of plaintiff's photograph without her written permission or consent to advertise the Minox camera was an invasion of her right of privacy under the New York statute. In Flores v. Mosler Safe Co. (164 NE2d 853, 1959) the defendant in the business of manufacturing and selling safes and vaults reprinted, in advertising its safes, an entire photograph and the original news coverage of a fire in which plaintiff's name was mentioned several times. The New York Court of Appeals had no difficulty in finding that this was a use of plaintiff's name for advertising purposes without his written permission. (The dissent argued that this public event was in the public domain and the use of plaintiff's name should not be actionable.)

In Schwartz v. Hebrew National, Inc., the New York Supreme Court, Queens County, on February 4, 1986, had occasion to consider the question whether it was essential that the plaintiff seeking damages for invasion of his right of privacy must also plead a demand for injunctive relief. Here plaintiff was an employee of a butcher shop (whose owner was deceased) when his photograph was taken by defendant product manufacturer; four years later the photograph was printed in the *New York Times* and the *Jewish Press* "without first obtaining from him a written or even a verbal release." Plaintiff contended that the printed photograph implied that he was the deceased owner of the butcher shop, causing plaintiff "severe emotional distress" to the tune of $1,000,000. But nowhere in his pleadings did plaintiff request injunctive relief which is available under Section 51 of the Civil Rights Law. A motion requesting a preliminary injunction was therefore denied, although the court softened the blow by concluding:

> Parenthetically this court is confident that defendants will voluntarily restrain from further use of the subject advertising photograph, since such allegedly unauthorized use would only further expose them to greater monetary damages including exemplary damages. A speedy trial can adequately resolve the dispute.

It is self-evident that courts have been careful to construe Sections 50 and 51 of the New York Civil Rights Law so as to fully protect the constitutional guarantees of free speech (Spahn v. Julian Messner, Inc., 286 NYS2d 832, 1967; cert den 393 US 1046, 1969). Courts will generally not apply Section 51 to grant injunctive relief to either a public figure or to one involved in a matter of public interest, unless plaintiff shows, in addition to the requirements of the New York statute, that the publication is materially and substantially false and was published with actual malice (Spahn v. Julian Messner, Inc., supra). The statute has been declared constitutional and not violative of either the federal or the state constitutions in that it does not deny persons the equal protection of the law and does not deprive them of liberty or property without due process of law, nor impair the obligations of contracts (Wyatt v. McCreery

& Co., 126 AD 650, 1908). The scope of the statute may be further summarized in these terms: (a) the right of privacy is a personal right which ends with the death of the individual (Lunceford v. Wilcox, 88 NYS2d 225, 1949); (b) there is no cause of action for the invasion of the right of privacy of another, no matter in what relationship plaintiff is to the other person (Schumann v. Loew's, Inc., 102 NYS2d 572, 1951); (c) the word "picture" is broad enough to include any representation of the person (Binns v. Vitagraph Corp., 211 NY 51, 1913); and (d) the term "advertising purposes" has been defined as "a solicitation for patronage" (Lahiri v. Daily Mirror, Inc., 162 Misc 776, 1937).

But Section 51 does set forth three situations in which the unauthorized use of a name or likeness is permissible, to wit: (1) a person, firm, or corporation practicing the profession of photography may exhibit in his, her, or its place of business examples of work done, unless and until the subject of the photography has objected in writing; (2) any person, firm, or corporation may use the name and likeness of any manufacturer or dealer in connection with any product that the manufacturer or dealer has sold or disposed of using his name or likeness; and (3) any person, firm, or corporation may use the name or likeness of any author, composer, or artist in connection with the literary, musical, or artistic productions which the author, composer, or artist has sold or disposed of using his name or likeness (Neyland v. Home Pattern Co., 65 F2d 363, 2nd Cir 1933).

In summary, it should be observed that New York does not formally recognize common law rights of privacy, and the only action based on a theory of invasion of privacy is under the aforementioned statute (Kiss v. Putnam County, 398 NYS2d 729, 1977). The absorbing case of Hill v. Erskine (240 NYS2d 286, 1963) is an example of the limitations on the right of privacy in New York under the statute. Here the publication of the novel *The Desperate Hours* by the defendant author constituted a violation of plaintiffs' right of privacy. Plaintiffs, husband and wife and their children, were held captive in their home for nineteen hours by three escaped convicts. Defendant about six months later published a novel about their experiences; later a play and motion picture were produced based upon the novel. Three years later, in 1955, after plaintiffs had moved to another state to forget about their bitter experience, the fictional play opened on Broadway. The adverse lower court decision was appealed by the publisher to the U.S. Supreme Court under the name Time, Inc. v. Hill (385 US 374, 1967), and the highest court in 1967 set aside the judgment in favor of the plaintiffs on the basis of First Amendment rights of the defendants. At the outset the court stressed that proof of knowing or reckless falsity was an essential ingredient to a constitutional application of the New York statute: "We hold that the constitutional protections for speech and press preclude the application of the New York statute to redress false reports of matters of public interest in the absence of proof that the defendant published the report with knowledge of its falsity or in reckless disregard of the truth." The court concluded:

We create a grave risk of serious impairment of the indispensable service of a free press in a free society if we saddle the press with the impossible burden of verifying to a certainty the facts associated in news articles with a person's name, picture or portrait, particularly as related to nondefamatory matter. Even negligence would be a most elusive standard, especially when the content of the speech itself affords no warning of prospective harm to another through falsity. A negligence test would place on the press the intolerable burden of guessing how a jury might assess the reasonableness of steps taken by it to verify the accuracy of every reference to a name, picture or portrait.

In this context, sanctions against either innocent or negligent misstatement would present a grave hazard of discouraging the press from exercising the constitutional guarantees. Those guarantees are not for the benefit of the press so much as for the benefit of all of us. A broadly defined freedom of the press assures the maintenance of our political system and an open society. Fear of large verdicts in damage suits for innocent or merely negligent misstatement, even fear of the expense involved in their defense, must inevitably cause publishers to steer . . . wider of the unlawful zone.

1.9 THE RIGHT OF PUBLICITY

The "right of publicity" is a concept which protects an individual's personality or personal dignity from appropriation by others for their economic benefit. It is a "right" that may be said to have evolved from the right of privacy. In Haelan Laboratories, Inc. v. Topps Chewing Gum, Inc. (102 F2d 866, 2nd Cir 1953) the Second U.S. Court of Appeals held that a person has "a right in the publicity value of his photograph, i.e., the right to grant the exclusive privilege of publishing his picture, and that such a grant may validly be made 'in gross,' i.e., without an accompanying transfer of a business or anything else. . . . This right might be called a 'right of publicity.' "

The form or element of the invasion of privacy cause of action closest to the "right of publicity" is the appropriation of name and likeness (see §2.2 herein), which is also incorporated in Section 652C of the Restatement (Second) of Torts. An individual need not be subject to the public exposure that widespread distribution of his or her name or likeness would produce. In Uhlaender v. Henricksen (316 F Supp 1277, Minn 1970) certain baseball players were granted injunctive relief without damages for the unauthorized use of their names. The U.S. Supreme Court in Zacchini v. Scripps-Howard Broadcasting Co. (443 US 562, 1977) recognized a performer's economic interest in his human cannonball act and spelled out the "right of publicity" under state law.

The "right of publicity," unlike the right of privacy, is apparently transferable or assignable in gross individuals while living. (See Estate of Elvis Presley v. Russen, 513 F Supp 1339, NJ 1981.) It appears that the "right of publicity" does not survive the death of the individual. In Memphis Development Foundation v. Factors, Etc., Inc. (616 F2d 956, 1980; cert den 449 US 953, 1980), the Sixth U.S. Court of Appeals, applying Tennessee law, ruled that making the "right of publicity" survive death would not enhance an individual's creative endeavors during his lifetime, nor would making the right inheritable increase the efficiency or productivity of the economic system nor increase the fairness of the economic or political system. In Lugosi v. Universal Pictures Co. (603 P2d 425, 1979) the California Supreme Court held that "the right to exploit name and likeness is personal to the artist and must be exercised, if at all, by him during his lifetime. . . . Neither society's interest in the free dissemination of ideas nor the artist's rights to the fruits of his own labor would be served by permitting the right to exploit artistic property which had not been exercised during the lifetime of the creator to survive his death." Accordingly, in Acme Circus Operating Co. v. Kuperstock (711 F2d 1538, 1983) the Eleventh U.S. Court of Appeals ruled that the late Clyde Beatty could license to buyers of his circus the right to use the name of Clyde Beatty and the Clyde Beatty Circus with all proceeds to Mrs. Beatty: "Where the right of publicity was exercised during the lifetime and turned into a commercial venture or other contract right, it becomes property that, under California law, survives and certainly may be assigned, giving the assignee the benefit of that assignment after the death of the assignor. . . . " In Estate of Elvis Presley v. Russen (supra) the federal district court in New Jersey opined that the right of publicity protected the interests of the deceased entertainer against imitation of his likeness and style of performance by another entertainer, and therefore the "right of publicity" survived his death.

The Georgia Supreme Court in Martin Luther King, Jr. Center for Social Change, Inc. v. American Heritage Productions, Inc. (296 SE2d 697, 1982) held that the "right of publicity" survived the death of its owner and was descendible irrespective of whether the right had been commercially exploited during the decedent's lifetime. The court wanted to halt the sale of plastic busts of Dr. King by the defendants at the expense of Dr. King's widow and the Center.

In Matter of Southeast Bank, N.A. v. Jack Lawrence, the New York Court of Appeals on November 26, 1985 (NYLJ, November 27, 1985, p. 1), called Florida law as controlling and thus gave a New York City theatre the right to name itself the Tennessee Williams Theatre. Under the New York conflict of laws rule personal property rights are determined by reference to the substantive law of the decedent's domicile, and under Florida law only one to whom a license has been issued during the decedent's lifetime and the decedent's surviving spouse and children possess a descendible right of publicity. It should be noted that "Tennessee Williams did not have a surviving spouse or child and did not issue a license during his lifetime," and therefore plaintiff here "possesses no enforceable property right." Accordingly, naming the theatre without the estate's consent did not violate the decedent's descendible "right of publicity."

Statutory recognition of the "right of publicity" is found in Tennessee (Tenn Code Ann Sec. 47-25-1101 and 47-25-1108), enacted in 1984, and in California (Cal Civ Code Sec. 990 and Sec. 3344), enacted in 1985. The states of Florida (Fla Stat Ann Sec. 540.80), Kentucky (Ky Rev Stat Sec. 191.179),

Oklahoma (Okla Stat Ann Sec. 839.170 or Title 21), Utah (Utah Code Ann Sec. 45-3-1 to Sec. 45-3-6), and Virginia (Va Code Sec 8.01-40) had enacted such legislation more than thirty-five years ago. Most statutes do not require that the plaintiff be a resident of the particular state, or that the "use" even take place within the state, or that the defendant be located in the state. The New York statute (Sections 50 and 51 of the New York Civil Rights Act; see §1.8 herein) requires that the "use" take place in New York, but there is no other territorial restriction on the parties. However, the New York and Virginia statutes have been held by the courts to preempt common law recovery for invasion of privacy, publicity, or misappropriation of name and likeness of a person. See Stephano v. News Group Publications, Inc. (485 NE2d 220, 1985), where plaintiff, a professional model, brought suit for violation of his statutory right to privacy when defendant published his pictures in a fashion article. Plaintiff alleged that he had agreed to model for one article only and that defendant violated that understanding by using his photograph for trade purposes without his consent. The trial court granted summary judgment for defendant, concluding that the article covered a newsworthy event in the fashion world and was not published for trade purposes. The appellate court reversed, finding that factual questions on "trade purposes" existed; but the New York Court of Appeals reversed, holding that the right of publicity is but an aspect of the purely statutory right of privacy in New York, and plaintiff could not claim a separate common law "right of publicity." The court found the article to fit within the newsworthiness exception to the New York statute; what is decisive is not defendant's motives to increase circulation of his paper, but the content of the news article. See also Evans v. Sturgill (530 F Supp 1209, WD Va 1977). The statutes of California, Kentucky, Florida, Tennessee, and Utah expressly provide that the statutory remedy is in addition to and not in derogation of all other rights, remedies, and causes of action. The state of Oklahoma's statute has permitted common law privacy actions (McCormack v. Oklahoma Publishing Co., 613 P2d 737, 1980). All of these state statutes, except New York's and Utah's, provide protection for names and likenesses of deceased individuals; however, Virginia limits the action up to twenty years, and California and Kentucky allow suit up to fifty years after death.

1.10 ELEMENTS OF THE INVASION OF PRIVACY CAUSE OF ACTION

The law of privacy, according to Professor William L. Prosser, comprises four distinct kinds of invasion of four distinct interests which are tied together by the common name of privacy, but which otherwise would have almost nothing in common except that each form of invasion of privacy represents an interference with the right of the person to be let alone. These forms of privacy may be identified as follows: (1) unreasonable intrusion or invasion by physical or mechanical means (see §2.1); (2) appropriation of name and likeness (see §2.2); (3) action putting person in false or unfavorable public light (see §2.3); and (4) public disclosure of private facts (see §2.7). These four elements are embodied in Section 652A of Restatement (Second) of Torts.

2

Invasions of Privacy: Protection of Individual Personal Dignity

2.1 UNREASONABLE INTRUSION OR INVASION BY PHYSICAL OR MECHANICAL MEANS

The first of Professor William L. Prosser's four distinct forms of the law of privacy concerns the unreasonable intrusion or invasion by physical or mechanical means. Under Section 652A of Restatement (Second) of Torts the right of privacy is invaded when there is "(a) unreasonable intrusion upon the seclusion of another. . . . " Section 652B then delineates that "one who intentionally intrudes, physically or otherwise, upon the solitude or seclusion of another, or his private affairs or concerns, is subject to liability to the other for invasion of his privacy, if the intrusion would be highly offensive to a reasonable man." Examples of such conduct include an illegal search of a person's shopping bag in a store (Sutherland v. Kroger Co., 110 SE2d 716, W. Va., 1959); eavesdropping upon private conversations by means of wiretapping (Hamberger v. Eastman, 206 A2d 239, N.H., 1964); peering into the windows of a home (Souder v. Pendleton Detectives, Inc., 88 So2d 716, La App, 1956); persistent and unwanted telephone calls (Harms v. Miami Daily News, Inc., 127 So2d 715, Fla, 1961); unauthorized prying into a person's bank account (Zimmerman v. Wilson, 81 F2d 847, 3rd Cir, 1936); and even an illegal blood test (Bednarik v. Bednarik, 16 A2d 80, N.J., 1940). Unauthorized entry onto private property, i.e., a trespass, may also serve as a basis for the action for unreasonable intrusion, as illustrated by Green Valley School, Inc. v. Cowles Florida Broadcasting, Inc. (327 So2d 810, Fla, 1976), where television reporters who accompanied police serving a warrant at a private school were found liable for invasion of privacy. In Engman v. Southwestern Bell Telephone Co. (591 SW2d

78, Mo App, 1979) and in Gonzalez v. Southwestern Bell Telephone Co. (555 SW2d 219, Tex App, 1977) telephone company employees entered the home of the plaintiffs to remove telephones after service had been terminated. In the Engman case the Missouri court ruled that the telephone company tariff, pursuant to which the company retained title to the telephones and authorized the company to enter the customers' premises to remove telephones, did not insulate the defendant telephone company from liability. In the Gonzalez case the fact that the plaintiffs were not at home at the time of the entry did not defeat plaintiff's claim of an invasion of their privacy.

The New Hampshire Supreme Court in Hamberger v. Eastman (supra) spelled out the elements of the cause of action for invasion of privacy in the defendant's installation and concealing in plaintiffs' bedroom a listening and recording device:

> The defendant contends that the right of privacy should not be recognized on the facts of the present case as they appear in the pleadings because there are no allegations that anyone listened or overheard any sounds or voices originating from the plaintiffs' bedroom. The tort of intrusion on the plaintiffs' solitude or seclusion does not require publicity and communication to third persons although this would affect the amount of damages. The defendant also contends that the right of privacy is not violated unless something has been published, written or printed and that oral publicity is not sufficient. Recent cases make it clear that this is not a requirement. . . .
>
> If the peeping Tom, the big ear and electronic eavesdropper (whether ingenious or ingenuous) have a place in the hierarchy of social values, it ought not to be at the expense of a married couple minding their own business in the seclusion of their bedroom who have never asked for or by their conduct deserved a potential projection of their private conversations and actions to their landlord or to others. Whether actual or potential such publicity with respect to private matters or purely personal concern is an injury to personality. It impairs the mental peace and comfort of the individual and may produce suffering more acute than that produced by a mere bodily injury. III Pound, Jurisprudence 58 (1959). The use of parabolic microphones and sonic wave devices designed to pick up conversations in a room without entering it and at a considerable distance away makes the problem far from fanciful. . . .
>
> It is unnecessary to determine the extent to which the right of privacy is protected as a constitutional matter without the benefit of statute. . . . For the purposes of the present case it is sufficient to hold that the invasion of the plaintiffs' solitude or seclusion, as alleged in the pleadings, was a violation of their right of privacy and constituted a tort for which the plaintiffs may recover damages to the extent that they can prove them. "Certainly, no right deserves greater protection, for, as Emerson has well said, 'solitude, the safeguard of mediocrity, is to genius the stern friend,' " Ezer, Intrusion on Solitude Herein of Civil Rights and Civil Wrongs, 21 Law in Transition 63, 75 (1961).

Physical intrusion which gives rise to invasion of privacy was the concern of the New York Court of Appeals in Nader v. General Motors Corp. (255 NE2d 765, 1970), which held that allegations that General Motors had engaged in overzealous surveillance of the well-known consumer advocate and had employed electronic eavesdropping equipment stated a claim for relief. However, other allegations of the plaintiff were deemed legally inadequate to support a claim for invasion of privacy, such as the assertions that General Motors had questioned acquaintances of the plaintiff and had cast aspersions on his views and his integrity and had caused women to accost him to entrap him into illicit sexual relations; these actions were deemed to be part of the offensive annoyances that permeate everyday life. In Spock v. U.S. (464 F Supp 510, SDNY, 1978) it was held that Dr. Spock stated a cause of action against the federal government for "alleged interception of oral, wire, telephone and telegraph communications." In another decision a federal district court in Hawaii awarded damages to an astronomer because CIA agents opened nineteen sealed envelopes representing correspondence by and to him from persons in the Soviet Union and intercepted two of his postcards (Cruikshank v. U.S., 467 F Supp 539, 1979). On the other hand, in Cassidy v. American Broadcasting Co. (377 NE2d 126, Ill, 1978) no intrusion occurred when a television station placed a camera behind a two-way mirror in a massage parlor to record an undercover police investigation of the establishment; the Illinois court found that, since the plaintiff was an on-duty police official, there was a legitimate interest in observing his behavior, and therefore the police official could have had no expectation of privacy in the pursuit of his official duties, aside from the defendant's legitimate pursuit of the news. The Sixth U.S. Court of Appeals in the 1984 decision in Boddie v. American Broadcasting Co. (731 F2d 333) dealt with the problem of hidden microphone interviews. Here a television program delineated allegations that an Ohio judge had regularly granted leniency to criminal defendants in exchange for sex. The plaintiff, an alleged participant in the scandal, had consented to be interviewed by defendant but refused to appear on camera. Unbeknown to plaintiff the interview was recorded both by concealed microphones and by a hidden videotape camera. The court found a cause of action under the Federal Wiretap Act based upon the allegation that plaintiff had an expectation that the interview was not being recorded by the camera.

Consent is an element in determining liability for intrusion, as shown in Barber v. Time, Inc. (159 SW2d 291, Mo, 1942). Here liability was imposed upon the magazine for printing the name and photograph of the plaintiff hospital patient, who had a rare glandular disorder which caused extreme obesity; the patient had consented to the interview but had wished to remain anonymous. The tort was completed when the photograph was taken since the plaintiff's consent was limited to the use of her words only. The Second U.S. Court of Appeals in Galella v. Onassis (487 F2d 986, 1973) ruled that Jacqueline Kennedy Onassis had given an implied consent to observation and news coverage of her activities by virtue of her status as a public figure; but that implied consent did not sanction the photographer harassing and interfering with her activities to the point where she and her children were terrified by the surreptitious methods employed by the photographer in invading her privacy. Consent was also exceeded in Le Mistral, Inc. v. Columbia Broadcasting System (402

NYS2d 815, 1978), where a television crew had "trespassed" into the restaurant to record on film the health code violations alleged by health inspectors; the consent of the restaurant, according to the court, was limited to persons who entered with intent to purchase food or drink, not to televise the interior of the restaurant.

The U.S. Supreme Court in Public Utility Commission v. Pollak (343 US 451, 1952) dealt with the problem of "an assault on the ears"; here the municipal bus and street railway system had provided "canned music" for the passengers on an eight-hour basis. Plaintiffs contended that the music "broadcasts" upon a "captive audience" were an "assault on the ears" and constituted an abuse of their privacy. The District of Columbia Circuit Court of Appeals (191 F2d 450, 1951) deemed the unreasonable invasion or intrusion a violation of the Fifth Amendment since the passengers were deprived of their liberty without due process of law; that court opined that the passengers were forced to hear the music instead of being free to "read, talk, meditate or relax." While such conduct can be abated under the guise of abating a private nuisance, the court pointed out that the transit company was a franchised monopoly authorized by government, and therefore the noise generated constituted a public nuisance which can be abated on constitutional grounds. In response to the transit carrier's defense of its right of free speech under the First Amendment, the court answered by quoting from Kovacs v. Cooper (336 US 77, 1949), to wit:

> The unwilling listener is not like the passerby who may be offered a pamphlet in the street but cannot be made to take it. In his home or on the street he is practically helpless to escape this interference with his privacy by loud speakers except through the protection of the municipality.

In 1949, in the Kovacs case, the highest court had upheld governmental regulation of loud and raucous sound trucks as non-violative of the right of free speech. But the U.S. Supreme Court did not agree with the appellate court, as the majority of the 1952 court in the Pollack case opined:

> The claim is that no matter how much Capital Transit may wish to use radio in its vehicles as part of its service to its passengers and as a source of income, no matter how much the great majority of its passengers may desire radio in those vehicles, and however positively the Commission, on substantial evidence may conclude that such use of radio does not interfere with the convenience, comfort and safety of the service but tends to improve it, yet if one passenger objects to the programs as an invasion of his constitutional right of privacy, the use of radio on the vehicles must be discontinued. This position wrongly assumes that the Fifth Amendment secures to each passenger on a public vehicle regulated by the Federal Government a right of privacy substantially equal to the privacy to which he is entitled in his own home. However complete his right of privacy may be at home, it is substantially limited by the rights of others when its possessor travels on a public thoroughfare or rides in a public conveyance.

Interestingly, Justice Felix Frankfurter declined to participate in the court's opinion since he found that he could not as a matter of fairness sit on a case where "his feelings were so strongly engaged as a victim of the practice in controversy." The dissent of Justice William O. Douglas lamented the fact that the passengers had no choice of the content of the music. (Years later the transit company discontinued the music broadcasting, which apparently the riding public never really liked.)

Implicit in this decision of the highest court in the Pollak case (supra) was an implied consent by the passengers, who voluntarily decided to ride the transit system with the music "assault" upon their ears. In a similar manner, the Florida Supreme Court in Florida Publishing Co. v. Fletcher (340 So2d 914, 1976) found "implied consent by custom." Here a newspaper had published a picture of a silhouette of the plaintiff's daughter, who had died in a fire at her home. When the fire occurred the photographer had entered the home with the fire marshall who was investigating the cause of the fire to photograph pertinent details. The court ruled that there was no trespass and that there was implied consent by custom. But in Rafferty v. Hartford Courant Co. (416 A2d 1215) the defendant news photographer, who was not invited to a mock "unwedding ceremony" at a private location (where the plaintiffs were celebrating their recent divorces), "crashed" the affair and later published the photographs, which publications were deemed to have invaded the privacy of the plaintiffs. The Connecticut court held that the public's right to know about the private acts of individuals was not absolute; and, in the absence of consent, implied or express, the publication of these private events was tortious. Telephone companies have been found liable for invasions of privacy when their employees entered customers' homes, even though the home may have been empty at the time, to repossess telephones used by customers who were delinquent in paying their bills (Gonzalez v. Southwestern Bell Telephone Co., 555 SW2d 219, 1977). A tenant in Lucas v. Ludwig (313 So2d 12, La App, 1975), who brought a police officer with her to reenter her old apartment to pick up her possessions that had been impounded by the landlord for nonpayment of rent, was held liable for invading the privacy of the landlord, to wit: the tenant, by causing the unwarranted police visit and police involvement, seriously interfered with the landlord's privacy in having the landlord's affairs known to others including the police, and thus the tenant went beyond any privilege or implied consent that the tenant may have had to enter the premises.

There can be a deliberate, unauthorized invasion of a plaintiff's privacy by non-physical means, as illustrated by Carey v. Statewide Finance Co. (223 A2d 405, Conn, 1966). Here defendant repeatedly telephoned the plaintiff at home and in the hospital to insist that she pay a debt owed by her husband; plaintiff suffered emotional distress which impaired her physical well-being. In Sistock v. Northwestern Telephone Systems (615 P2d 176, 1980) the Montana Supreme Court reversed a trial court's finding that the telephone company had not invaded plaintiff's privacy by recording plaintiff's telephone conversations for six days after the company had received complaints by subscribers to the line. The court deemed the question of invasion of privacy to be one for the jury to decide under all the circumstances of the case. An intrusion should take place on private premises, for on a public street or in any public place plaintiff has no legal right to be alone (Forster v. Manchester, 189 A2d 147, Pa, 1963). But, even in a public place, there are some matters which are still private, so that a woman who is photographed with her dress unexpectedly blown up in a "fun house" has a cause of action for invasion of privacy (Daily Times Democrat Co. v. Graham, 162 So2d 474, Ala, 1964). The means utilized and the purpose for which the intrusion was made are indeed important factors in determining whether liability can be predicated. See McLain v. Boise Cascade Corp. (533 P2d 343, Ore, 1975) and Marks v. Bell Telephone Co. (331 A2d 424, 1975); in the latter case a city in Pennsylvania had installed a telephone recording system in its jail, and the conversation of the plaintiff, an attorney, with his client, a prisoner, was recorded; but the Pennsylvania court found no cause of action for invasion of privacy on the ground that the recordings were never replayed: "The only ear ever to hear appellant's communication was a mechanical one."

Intrusion upon plaintiff's solitude must be "highly offensive to a reasonable person" within the definition of Section 652B of Restatement (Second) of Torts, as shown in Froelich v. Adair (516 P2d 993, Kan, 1973). Here the defendant in a pending libel action brought by her former husband had a friend obtain from a hospital room occupied by the male plaintiff samples of the plaintiff's hair from a hairbrush and from a discarded adhesive bandage. The hair samples would prove the truth of the alleged libel that defendant's former husband had a homosexual affair with the male plaintiff. The Kansas court deemed the conduct of the defendant (and her friend) to constitute an invasion of the privacy of the male plaintiff; the dissenting opinion argued that the intrusion would not be "highly offensive to a reasonable person," particularly in a private room with no one present.

Obtaining information through improperly intrusive means, even if that information is not published, is still an actionable tort, as illustrated by Pearson v. Dodd (410 F2d 701, DC Cir, 1969; cert den 395 US 947, 1969). Here two nationally syndicated columnists, Drew Pearson and Jack Anderson, had sanctioned the obtaining of information about a U.S. Senator through ex-employees of the U.S. Senator who entered the official office, removed certain official files, copied other files, and turned over the fruits of their labors to the two columnists, both of whom were aware of the surreptitious means employed. The U.S. Senator sued the columnists for invasion of privacy and conversion of the documents. But the court determined that only the ex-employees of the U.S. Senator, not the two columnists, were guilty of the invasion of privacy. It is submitted that the two columnists would not have been guilty of invasion of privacy if the information of legitimate concern to the public so obtained had in fact been published; Section 652D of Restatement (Second) of Torts provides:

> One who gives publicity to a matter concerning the private life of another is subject to liability to the other for invasion of his privacy, if the matter publicized is of a kind that (a) would be highly offensive to a reasonable person, and (b) is not of legitimate concern to the public.

A more subtle form of intrusion occurred in People v. Hollman, decided December 10, 1985, by the New York Supreme Court, Appellate Term, for the Second and Eleventh Judicial Districts: "The right to privacy is essentially the right to be left alone. . . . [it] does not create the right to impose one's lifestyle on others who have an equal right to be left alone." The issue was the constitutionality of a New York Penal Law prohibition against nude bathing in public places. The court ruled that the 1983 New York statute was a proper legislative action that did not undermine First Amendment rights such as the right to privacy, inter alia. Quoting Chapin v. Town of Southampton (457 F Supp 1170, EDNY, 1978), the court opined that "the right to appear au naturel at home is relinquished when one sets foot on a public sidewalk. . . . Nor should the right of privacy be extended to protect nude bathing. . . . The desire of a group to sunbathe nude does not without more raise a constitutional right in that group to associate nude on a public beach."

In reviewing this first element of unreasonable intrusion or invasion of the right of privacy, it appears that there are (a) gratuitous and even wanton intrusions; (b) indiscriminate invasions; and (c) intrusions without safeguards against control or supervision of the security of the information or data. The first category (a) would embrace such gratuitous intrusions that serve no legitimate purpose, perhaps being mere items of idle curiosity or of a malicious prankster; those intrusions that are unnecessary because less intrusive means are available to obtain the needed information or data, i.e., telephoning rather than wiretapping; and those intrusions which are arbitrary and capricious in the sense that an entire organization is put under electronic surveillance so as to root out the one guilty person. The second category (b) delineated as indiscriminate invasions would include those that acquire information that is not relevant, such as electronic surveillance of wholly innocent people at a toilet facility so as to single out homosexuals, and those intrusions that are performed by disclosing information of a highly sensitive nature about a person in order to alert certain persons about that person's presence. The third category (c) deals with failures to enforce suitable safeguards which would preclude valuable and personal information from falling into the wrong hands, as where data compiled by computer technology are not kept under lock and key. It is obvious that if society is to guard against violations of the right of privacy in the form of unreasonable intrusions, emphasis must be placed upon such factors as the following: there must be a valid or legitimate need for invading privacy; there must be probable cause as to the relevancy of the required information or data; there must be no reasonable alternative for acquiring the data, which alternative is less intrusive; and there must be restricitons on access to the data under proper security measures.

On this issue of security measures that must be taken to protect against intrusions and invasions of privacy, the U.S. Supreme Court in Whalen v. Roe (429 US 589, 1976) gave finite answers. Here the state of New York had required by statute that the names and addresses of all persons obtaining such drugs as opium, cocaine, amphetamines, and other drugs for which there is both a lawful and an unlawful use be kept on public record on magnetic tapes stored in a vault for five years. A locked fence and alarm system provided security for the information processing system, for public disclosure of the identified persons was prohibited. The highest court unanimously found that the New York legislation authorizing this entire procedure did not infringe upon the identified person's privacy:

> We are not unaware of the threat to privacy implied in the accumulation of vast amounts of personal information in computerized data banks or other massive government files. The collecting of taxes, the distribution of welfare and social security benefits, the supervision of public health, the direction of the armed forces and the enforcement of the criminal laws all require the orderly preservation of great quantities of information, much of which is personal in nature and potentially embarrassing or harmful if disclosed. The right to collect and use such data for public purposes is typically accompanied by a concomitant statutory or regulatory duty to avoid unwarranted disclosures.

The highest court demonstrated great sensitivity to the privacy needs of an information-based society and was satisfied that a "carefully designed program with numerous safeguards intended to forestall the danger of indiscriminate disclosure" would protect privacy for legitimate state purposes. The New York statute, without its privacy safeguards, could have identified law-abiding citizens as users of illicit drugs, jeopardizing their employment and community standing.

In U.S. v. U.S. District Court (407 US 297, 1972) the same highest court had solemnized that "our task is to examine and balance the basic values at stake," weighing "the duty of Government to protect the domestic security and the potential danger posed by unreasonable surveillance to individual privacy. . . ." In U.S. v. Miller (425 US 435, 1976) the petitioner was defeated on expectation of privacy grounds when he challenged the admissibility of microfilmed evidence of checks, deposit slips, and other records obtained by subpoena to the two banks maintaining the records. The court viewed the microfilm as bank business records rather than as private papers, and found no Fourth Amendment violation of privacy. The conclusion of the court was that there was no expectation of privacy in the negotiable instruments; thus, the court was unwilling to expand the privacy right to modern needs. Probably the court was even more hostile to the petitioner's effort to quash evidence of his clear criminality.

One final point on the scope of unreasonable intrusion or invasion of privacy, to wit: a loss of privacy occurs whenever a plaintiff institutes legal action. As stated in U.S. v. Hubbard (650 F2d 293, DC Cir, 1980), "the mere institution of litigation greatly accentuates the original loss of privacy; in fact, it normally multiplies the very effect from which relief is sought." The point is simply that a plaintiff may not subsequently be heard to complain of an intrusion upon his privacy; an injured plaintiff's private life cannot remain private in an open court of law. In theory, at least, only the most outrageous invasions of privacy should reach the litigation state.

2.2 APPROPRIATION OF NAME AND LIKENESS

Another distinct form of the law of privacy is the appropriation of the name and likeness of the plaintiff for the benefit or advantage of the defendant. See 55 *Northwestern Univ. Law Review* 553 (1961). Section 652C of Restatement (Second) of Torts states that "one who appropriates to his own use or benefit the name or likeness of another is subject to liability to the other for invasion of his privacy." This form is readily distinguishable from other forms of privacy in that it does not involve the individual's right to be left alone; indeed, the myriad misappropriation cases delineate commercial situations where the plaintiff's name or likeness or photograph is used without his consent in a manner suggesting or implying that plaintiff has endorsed or approved the particular product. The earliest privacy case, Pavesich v. New England Life Insurance Co. (50 SE 68), in 1905 concerned the defendant insurance company utilizing plaintiff's name, photograph, and false testimonial in its advertising campaign. In Spellman v. Simon & Schuster Co., the New York appellate court in 1978 upheld a jury verdict to the effect that the defendant publisher had used without permission a photograph of a black high school student on a book cover in order to attract the attention of young black readers and sell more books.

In New York, under Sections 50 and 51 of the New York Civil Rights Law (see §1.8 herein), limits are placed on the scope of the appropriation of name and likeness, to wit: use for advertising or for "purposes of trade" and lack of written consent are the controlling terms. In Caesar v. Chemical Bank the New York Court of Appeals on October 17, 1985, emphasized that the right of privacy exists in New York solely as a matter of statute; the bank was held liable for the use of a photograph of its own employees because there was no written consent and neither oral nor implied consent could justify the bank's conduct in using the photograph. Here a class action suit was instigated by employees, and the success of the plaintiffs here served to confirm that in New York the only cause of action for invasion of privacy is in the statute on appropriation of name and likeness. The use of a celebrity look-alike in an advertisement of a product would constitute a violation of the statute (Onassis v. Christian Dior, 472 NYS2d 254, 1984).

While ''appropriation'' cases depend on the premise that people have property rights in their lives and personal activities, a concern for societal values also underlies the decisions of courts. In Zacchini v. Scripps-Howard Broadcasting Co. (433 US 562, 1977) a sharply divided U.S. Supreme Court held that the First Amendment did not bar a performer's claim for damages against a television station that had telecast a film of his entire act. Justice Byron R. White commented that the ''right of publicity'' here ''rests on more than a desire to compensate the performer for the time and effort invested in his act; the protection provides an economic incentive for him to make the investment required to produce a performance of interest to the public.'' In such situations the judicial decisions are said to respond more to mores and to condition social choice-making. But in Venturi v. Savitt, Inc. (191 Conn 588, 1983) the plaintiff, a professional golfer, had posed for a photograph with the defendant during a local golf tournament in 1963; in 1973 plaintiff, then a sportscaster, found that this same photograph was used as an advertisement to sell the 1973 local golf tournament. The Connecticut court found no evidence of damages, either compensatory or punitive, and ruled that there was no invasion of privacy. Similarly, in Majka v. Bristol Press Publishing Co., the Connecticut Superior Court ruled that a newspaper's publication without plaintiff's consent of a photograph of plaintiff walking along a public street did not constitute an invasion of privacy. The standard applied was that of reasonableness and not the subjective feelings of the individual. And yet in 1959 the Connecticut court in Korn v. Rennison (156 A2d 476) had opined:

> The line to be drawn between reasonable demands of individual privacy and public interest in legitimate news is not always easy to define, but the boundary is more readily perceived in the case of commercial advertising. . . . No case decided within the last fifteen years has been found in which the existence of a right of privacy has been denied.

Here a photograph of the plaintiff was published for advertising purposes in the defendant newspaper without the knowledge, consent, or permission of the plaintiff and allegedly in violation of her personal liberties and private rights. The plaintiff was a minor, and the court was of the opinion that the minor was offended by the photograph, which fact the defendant should have known. However, the 1964 Connecticut decision of Stedding v. Battistoni (208 A2d 559) corrected that opinion by holding that the essential element of privacy misappropriation is the unauthorized use of the plaintiff's name or likeness for the defendant's benefit; the defendant need not be aware that its use of plaintiff's name or likeness would be offensive to the plaintiff, if defendant gains a benefit or advantage therefrom.

Publication of one's photograph for the defendant's benefit is illustrated by

Falke v. Greensboro News Co. (195 NE 55, 1938). Here the newspaper ran an advertisement for a vaudeville show and mistakenly used a photograph of the plaintiff wearing a bathing suit, believing the photograph was that of the leading lady in the vaudeville show. The North Carolina Supreme Court declared that "security of person is as necessary as the security of property" and likened the unauthorized use of plaintiff's photograph for commercial gain of the defendant newspaper to the unauthorized publication of one's lecture or commercial drawing: "An act of invasion of the individual's privacy results, possibly more formidable and more painful in its consequences than an actual bodily assault might be." Generally defendant's benefits must be pecuniary, although in non-statutory states, "political gain" has been recognized, as shown in Hinish v. Meier & Frank Co. (113 P2d 438, Ore, 1941). But the mere incidental mention of plaintiff's name in a book or a motion picture is not an invasion of his privacy (University of Notre Dame v. Twentieth Century Fox Film Corp., 256 NYS2d 301, 1965; aff 259 NYS2d 832, 1965). However, parody may result in actionable misappropriation, as illustrated by Lombardo v. Doyle, Dane & Birnbach, Inc. (396 NYS2d 661, 1977), which held that the famous orchestra leader, Guy Lombardo, had an actionable claim against the advertising agency which had imitated his public personality, "Mr. New Year's Eve," in an advertisement of a product. Also, in Ali v. Playgirl, Inc. (447 F Supp 723, DC, 1978), the federal district court granted a preliminary injunction against the further distribution of a magazine containing an illustration of a nude black athlete which was clearly identifiable as the plaintiff boxer; an accompanying verse entitled "The Greatest" imitated plaintiff's poetic style and described his sexual powers. Increasing the circulation of the magazine was the benefit sought by the defendant to the detriment of the plaintiff. In Carson v. Here's Johnny Portable Toilets, Inc. (698 F2d 831, 6th Cir, 1983) the court held that the entertainer Johnny Carson has a right not to have his name appropriated, but plaintiff had no recourse about his embarrassment from being associated with defendant's portable toilets. On the other hand, in Cordell v. Detective Publications, Inc. (419 F2d 989, 6th Cir, 1969) the magazine's unauthorized and sensational account of the murder of plaintiff's daughter did not give rise to any cause of action under Tennessee law because the references to plaintiff could not "reasonably be interpreted as casting her in public disrepute, nor could they reasonably be offensive or objectionable to a person of ordinary sensibilities as they reflect on Mrs. Cordell." It should be noted that the name or likeness must have commercial value to serve as the basis for appropriation by the defendant (Lawrence v. A. S. Abell Co., 475 A2d 448, Md, 1984).

2.3 ACTION PUTTING PLAINTIFF IN FALSE OR UNFAVORABLE PUBLIC LIGHT

A third form of invasion of privacy consists of publicity which places the plaintiff in a false light in the public eye. The earliest case was the 1816 English decision in Lord Byron v. Johnston (35 Eng Rep 851), when Lord Byron succeeded in enjoining the circulation of a bad poem that had been attributed to him. The very action putting plaintiff in false or unfavorable public light must be judged from the viewpoint of the reasonable person. The entry of an actor without his consent in a popularity contest of an embarrassing kind (Marks v. Jaffa, 26 NYS 908, 1893) or the inclusion of the plaintiff's name, photograph, or fingerprints in a public "rogue's gallery" of convicted criminals when plaintiff has not in fact been convicted of any crime (Itzkovitz v. Whitaker, 39 So 499, 1950) are examples of a "false light" that would be highly offensive to a reasonable person. The tort is defined in Section 652E of Restatement (Second) of Torts as follows:

> One who gives publicity to a matter concerning another that places the other before the public in a false light is subject to liability to the other for invasion of his privacy, if (a) the false light in which the other was placed would be highly offensive to a reasonable person, and (b) the actor had knowledge of or acted in reckless disregard as to the falsity of the publicized matter and the false light in which the other would be placed.

It would appear that the "false light" action is intended to compensate for injury to feelings rather than reputation, and that the plaintiff must prove actual malice. However, the Fifth U.S. Court of Appeals in Wood v. Hustler Magazine, Inc., in 1984 held that the magazine publisher could be held liable for *negligently* placing a private person in a false light. In Braun v. Flynt the same court in 1984 held that the plaintiff had proved the elements of her "false light" privacy claim because the overall impression which the magazine conveyed of her was false. But the court here found that plaintiff was not a public figure and that the magazine had indeed acted with actual malice in obtaining and in publishing her picture. *Hustler Magazine* received a similar blow in Douglass v. Hustler Magazine, Inc., when the U.S. Supreme Court on April 1, 1986, refused to review a ruling of the Seventh U.S. Court of Appeals that had reversed the trial court's award of $600,000 to the plaintiff actress and had ordered a new trial due to both errors at trial and excessive damages awarded by the federal district court jury. It appears that plaintiff actress' nude picture had appeared first in *Playboy Magazine* with her permission and then subsequently appeared in defendant's magazine without her permission. The federal appellate court found that she had a cause of action for being portrayed in a "false light," and it was this determination that prompted Hustler Magazine, Inc. to appeal to the U.S. Supreme Court. The new trial would therefore be limited to the issue of the measure of damages. In Annerino v. Dell Publishing Co. (149 NE2d 616, 1958) the plaintiff wife of a slain police officer was the subject of an article in defendant's magazine three months later. The article was entitled "If You Love Me, Slip Me a Gun" and with the subtitles "She Lifted Her Ballerina Skirt: There, Honey, Fastened to the Garter." The Illinois court agreed that the article posited plaintiff in a false light, and implied that malice motivated the defendant magazine by virtue of the fact that the article was written as an appeal to idle and prurient interest. But in Meetze v. Associated Press (95 SE2d 606, 1956) the South Carolina court found no invasion of privacy in the newspaper story of a twelve-year-old bride who delivered a child exactly twelve months after the marriage. The court ruled that for a twelve-year-old girl to give birth to a child is a biological occurrence naturally exciting public interest, and the publication of facts about it could not be an invasion of a right of privacy. Similarly, in Virgil v. Time, Inc. (527 F2d 1122, 1975), the Ninth U.S. Court of Appeals found no invasion of privacy; here the defendant published an article about daredevil body surfers and included in a profile of the plaintiff a description of some of his bizarre behaviorisms, such as burning holes in his hand with cigarettes to impress women, throwing himself downstairs to collect disability benefits, and eating spiders to demonstrate his manliness. The defense of newsworthiness was upheld:

> In determining what is a matter of legitimate public interest, account must be taken of the customs and conventions of the community; and in the last analysis what is proper becomes a matter of the community mores. The line is to be drawn when the publicity ceases to be the giving of information to which the public is entitled, and becomes a morbid and sensational prying into private lives for its own sake, with which a reasonable member of the public, with decent standards, would say he had no concern.

On remand, the federal district court granted summary judgment to the defendant, holding that the revelations did not constitute "morbid and sensational prying into private lives," and that, even if one could find such prying, it was done to explain the character of a local hero and not "for its own sake."

There are three major categories of the "false light" privacy tort, to wit: embellishment, distortion, and fictionalization; see §2.4, §2.5, and §2.6 herein. The state of California's Supreme Court has stated that a "false light" invasion of privacy is "in substance . . . the equivalent" of a libel claim and should meet the same requirements (Johnson v. Harcourt Brace Jovanovich, Inc., 43 Cal App3d 880, 1974). But the majority view is that the "false light" claim need not be a defamatory one, although it very often is (Russell v. Marboro Books, 183 NYS2d 8, 1959).

2.4 EMBELLISHMENT

Embellishment is the process of adding false material to an otherwise truthful story, and thereby placing the plaintiff in a "false light." In Cantrell v. Forest City Publishing Co. (419 US 245, 1974) the U.S. Supreme Court reviewed the newspaper article describing the effect upon the widow and son following the death of the husband in a bridge collapse. The widow was delineated as "wearing the same mask of non-expression she wore at her husband's funeral," when in fact the newspaper had not interviewed the widow for the follow-up article.

The court ruled that such embellishment constituted a "false light" claim for invasion of privacy. The dissenting opinion of Justice Douglas was grounded upon freedom of the press:

> An accident with a bridge catapulted the Cantrells into the public eye and their disaster became newsworthy. To make the First Amendment freedom to report the news turn on subtle differences between common-law malice and actual malice is to stand the Amendment on its head. Those who write the current news seldom have the objective, dispassionate point of view—or the time—of scientific analysts. They deal in fast moving events and the need for "spot" reporting. The jury under today's formula sits as a censor with broad powers—not to impose a prior restraint but to lay heavy damages on the press. The press is "free" only if the jury is sufficiently disenchanted with the Cantrells to let the press be free of this damage claim. The regime is thought by some to be a way of supervising the press which is better than not supervising it at all. But the installation of the Court's regime would require a constitutional amendment. Whatever might be the ultimate reach of the doctrine Justice Black and I have embraced, it seems clear that in matters of public import such as the present news reporting, there must be freedom from damages lest the press be frightened into playing a more ignoble role than the Framers visualized.

It was in the same spirit of defending the freedom of the press that the Reverend Jerry Falwell was unsuccessful in his suit against *Penthouse Magazine* for publishing an interview with him. In Falwell v. Penthouse International, Ltd. (521 F Supp 1204, 1981) the federal district court in West Virginia, applying West Virginia law, found no embellishment that could amount to invasion of the right of privacy; furthermore, a cause of action based on "false light" could not be maintained in the state. The Arkansas Supreme Court in Dodrill v. Arkansas Democrat Co. (590 SW2d 840, 1979) also found nothing wrong about publishing the fact that a recently suspended lawyer had not passed the bar examination, which was a condition precedent to reinstatement of his license to practice law. And in Cape Publications, Inc. v. Bridges (423 So2d 426, 1982) the Florida appellate court declared that "where one becomes an actor in an occurrence of public interest, it is not an invasion of her right of privacy to publish her photograph with an account of such occurrence." The defendant published a story concerning the abduction and holding as hostage of a woman plaintiff by her estranged husband, including the publication of a photograph of the female plaintiff escaping, clad only in a dish towel.

A question of embellishment was implicit in the famous case of Sidis v. F-R Publishing Corp. (113 F2d 806, 2nd Cir, 1940). According to the court:

> William James Sidis was a famous child prodigy in 1910. His name and prowess were well known to newspaper readers of the period. At the age of eleven, he lectured to distinguished mathematicians on the subject of Four-Dimensional Bodies. When he was sixteen, he was graduated from Harvard College, amid considerable public attention. Since then, his name has appeared in the press only sporadically, and he has sought to

live as unobtrusively as possible. Until the articles objected to appeared in the *New Yorker*, he had apparently succeeded in his endeavor to avoid the public gaze.

Among the *New Yorker*'s features are brief biographical sketches of current and past personalities. In the latter department, which appears haphazardly under the title of "Where Are They Now?" the article on Sidis was printed with a subtitle "April Fool." The author describes his subject's early accomplishments in mathematics and the widespread attention he received, then recounts his general breakdown and the revulsion which Sidis thereafter felt for his former life of fame and study. The unfortunate prodigy is traced over the years that followed, through his attempts to conceal his identity, through his chosen career as an insignificant clerk who would not need to employ unusual mathematical talents, and through the bizarre ways in which his genius flowered, as in his enthusiasm for collecting streetcar transfers and in his proficiency with an adding machine. The article closes with an account of an interview with Sidis at his present lodgings, "a hall bedroom of Boston's shabby south end." The untidiness of his room, his curious laugh, his manner of speech, and other personal habits are commented upon at length, as is his present interest in the lore of the Okamakammessett Indians. The subtitle is explained by the closing sentence, quoting Sidis as saying "with a grin" that it was strange, "but, you know, I was born on April Fool's Day." Accompanying the biography is a small cartoon showing the genius of eleven years lecturing to a group of astounded professors.

The Second U.S. Court of Appeals ruled that defendant's article "sketched the life of an unusual personality, and it possessed considerable popular news interest. . . . And when such are the mores of the community, it would be unwise for a court to bar the expression in newspapers, books and magazines of the day." In essence, the court, finding no embellishment, held that "once a public figure, always a public figure."

2.5 DISTORTION

Another category of the "false light" privacy claim is distortion, which involves intentional falsity in either the context of the material or the omission of certain relevant facts. In Jumez v. ABC Records, Inc., the federal district court in New York in 1978 sustained a jury verdict under the New York Civil Rights Law where the defendant record company had placed a picture of a bearded, half-naked man (whom defendant knew not to be the guitarist) on the cover of the plaintiff guitarist's record album. On the other hand, the Iowa Supreme Court in Bremmer v. Journal-Tribune Publishing Co. (76 NW2d 762, 1956) published a large picture of the public site where plaintiffs' son's body was found, mutilated and decomposed. The court conceded that the incident of finding the body of the missing local boy was one of "proper public interest." In other words, the event was newsworthy, and there was no distortion placing the boy in false light. The dissent of Chief Justice Larson argued that plaintiffs should have been allowed to show "what might be termed was an indecent picture of the boy's body":

I am not advocating that the courts or anyone else try to act as censors of the press, but who will protect the invaded rights of citizens if the courts do not? It is not censoring, as I view it, to provide a remedy for a wrong, once the wrong has been done.

It is my feeling that we should take this opportunity to clearly express a sound position on this important question. We should recognize the right of privacy by more than lip service. We should limit and define the privilege accorded the press and radio to invade this right of individual privacy here in Iowa. It must be done sometime. This is not a new thought, for in Prosser on Torts, 2d Ed., pages 643–644, we find the following statement:

> Again the privilege is not unlimited, but the line is a most difficult one to draw. The cases in which the privilege has been found to be exceeded have involved outrageous methods such as the theft of a photograph, or extreme catering to the morbid and the sensational, such as the publication of the picture of the plaintiff's dead, deformed child, . . . The best statement that can be made is that the distinction probably is that found in other cases of the intentional infliction of mental suffering, between conduct which outrages the common decencies and goes beyond what the public mores will tolerate, and that which the plaintiff must be expected under the circumstances to endure.

Clearly, then, the privilege of the publisher is not absolute. But because the line is difficult to draw, we should not try to avoid it this way. We are constantly called upon to draw distinctions just as difficult, and we try to do so for the benefit of bench and bar. I would reverse this judgment and order the trial court to at least hear and see the evidence before determining, under such guidance as we can provide at this time, whether or not as a matter of law defendant did breach the privilege to invade plaintiffs' right of privacy extended to it under these circumstances.

The right of the press to publish photographs of the gruesome effects of an atrocious crime was upheld by the Georgia Supreme Court in Waters v. Fleetwood (91 SE2d 344, 1956). On the other hand, in Taylor v. KTVB, Inc. (525 P2d 984, 1974), the Idaho Supreme Court was more sympathetic to the plight of the plaintiff, who was arrested and taken from his home while in the nude. The defendant television station telecast the event, and plaintiff's buttocks and genitals were clearly visible to television viewers. The court held that the use of material of a highly offensive nature would be actionable if done for the purpose of embarrassing or humiliating the plaintiff, and it was up to the jury to make the determination of distortion, if any.

In Quiles v. Public Broadcasting Service, dated January 9, 1986, the New York Supreme Court, New York County, reviewed a television film portraying a Spanish Harlem family in what plaintiffs deemed to be a ''false light.'' The film showed plaintiffs as a drug-addicted family actively selling marijuana. The court granted defendant's summary judgment motion:

> Even assuming that the ''false light'' test exists in New York, and that these plaintiffs could conceivably, on this record—including their own admissions of drug use—be said to have been presented in a false light; and assuming further that the ''gross irrespon-

sibility,'' rather than the ''actual malice,'' standard is applicable and even if there actually was some oral understanding between the plaintiffs and the producers—nevertheless the false light test would still be inapplicable here because of the lack of any proof that the public television defendants knew of, or acted irresponsibly with respect to, any of the alleged falsities. Karaduman v. Newsday, Inc. (51 NY2d 531, 1930). The letter from the Livingston Manor lawyer said nothing about falsity, but merely mentioned the alleged lack of consent—and even that letter was sent a year after the first broadcast, and two weeks before the second; the falsity issue was not actually raised until the federal complaint in November 1984. Moreover, plaintiffs do not even claim that defendants knew of the alleged agreement as to the five-year wait or plaintiffs' right of approval of cuts (assuming the truth of these unlikely conditions).

Finally, although there was no need to do so, defendants did in fact immediately check with the producers, and were assured that there was no merit to the charge, that all consents had been obtained and all participants paid at least regular minimum wages. Broadcasters must be able to rely on the reputation of producers of films, the review of those films by their own news and public affairs departments, and the willingness of the producers to guaranty that consent was obtained; otherwise, any letter claiming falsity or lack of consent could effectively stop any program the writer did not like, and thus would burden broadcasters so much as to have a chilling effect on First Amendment rights.

2.6 FICTIONALIZATION

Fictionalization occurs as an invasion of privacy, where actual people appear as characters in fictional works, unless the actual people are public figures or the events involve matters of public concern. In Prytash v. Best Medium Publishing Co. (254 A2d 872, 1969) the Connecticut court observed that the defendant accidentally published plaintiff's picture in a story concerning different women who had abandoned their babies and were subsequently arrested on felony charges; the court awarded damages to the plaintiff on the basis of fictionalization, amounting to putting plaintiff in a ''false light.''

In Melvin v. Reid (297 P91, 1931) plaintiff's complaint alleged that she was a former prostitute who was tried and acquitted of murder. She thereupon ''abandoned her life of shame'' and a year later married and ''assumed a place in respectable society.'' Seven years after her acquittal the defendants released a motion picture accurately depicting her earlier life and using her unmarried name. The motion picture, according to plaintiff, informed her friends for the first time of the unsavory incidents of her past. The California Court of Appeal found an invasion of her privacy by defendant's use of her real name and not a fictionalization: ''All men . . . have certain inalienable rights, among which are those of . . . pursuing and obtaining . . . happiness,'' and plaintiff's ''right'' had been violated by the publication. Forty years later the California Supreme Court in Briscoe v. Reader's Digest Association (483 P2d, 34, 1971) echoed the same view:

We are realistic enough to recognize that men are curious about the inner sanctums of their neighbors—that the public will create its heroes and villains. We must also be realistic enough to realize that full disclosure of one's inner thoughts, intimate personal characteristics, and past life is neither the rule nor the norm in these United States. We have developed a variegated panoply of professional listeners to whom we confidentially "reveal all"; otherwise we keep our own counsel. The masks we wear may be stripped away upon the occurrence of some event of public interest. But just as the risk of exposure is a concomitant of urban life, so too is the expectation of anonymity regained. It would be a crass legal fiction to assert that a matter once public never becomes private again. Human forgetfulness over time puts today's "hot" news in tomorrow's dusty archives. In a nation of 200 million people there is ample opportunity for all but the most infamous to begin a new life.

Plaintiff is a man whose last offense took place 11 years before, who has paid his debt to society, who has friends and an 11 year old daughter who were unaware of his early life—a man who has assumed a position in "respectable" society. Ideally, his neighbors should recognize his present worth and forget his past life of shame. But men are not so divine as to forgive the past trespasses of others and plaintiff therefore endeavored to reveal as little as possible of his past life. Yet, as if in some bizarre canyon of echoes, petitioner's past life pursues him through the pages of Reader's Digest, now published in 13 languages and distributed in 100 nations, with a circulation in California alone of almost 2,000,000 copies.

In a nation built upon the free dissemination of ideas, it is always difficult to declare that something may not be published. But the great general interest in an unfettered press may at times be outweighed by other great societal interests. As a people we have come to recognize that one of these societal interests is that of protecting an individual's right to privacy. The right to know and the right to have others not know are, simplistically considered, irreconcilable. But the rights guaranteed by the First Amendment do not require total abrogation of the right of privacy. The goals sought by each may be achieved with a minimum of intrusion upon the other. . . .

We do not hold today that plaintiff must prevail in his action. It is for the trier of fact to determine (1) whether plaintiff had become a rehabilitated member of society, (2) whether identifying him as a former criminal would be highly offensive and injurious to the reasonable man, (3) whether defendant published this information with a reckless disregard for its offensiveness, and (4) whether any independent justification for printing plaintiff's identity existed. We hold today only that, as pleaded, plaintiff has stated a valid cause of action, sustaining the demurrer to plaintiff's complaint was improper, and that the ensuing judgment must therefore be reversed.

Earlier, in 1954, the New York court in People v. Chas. Scribner & Sons, Inc. (205 Misc 818) was concerned about a criminal complaint against the book publisher of *From Here to Eternity* (which was subsequently made into a motion picture). The novel delineated life at an army post in Hawaii just before the Pearl Harbor catastrophe; the complainant was Joseph Anthony Maggio, whose name closely resembled the fictional character in the book, "Angelo Maggio." The court found no invasion of privacy since there was no positive identification of the complainant with the fictional character; nor was the complainant's name or likeness used without his permission. The court opined that it was within the bounds of legal propriety to employ any nomenclature in a work of fiction as long as there was no description or characterization of personal, public, and familial fact which would identify the complainant to the reader: "It is obvious that there is always the possibility that, no matter what name is used, there is always some living person with that name." Similarly, in James v. Screen Gems, Inc. (344 P2d 799), the California court held that the alleged invasion of privacy of a third person was not actionable by his relatives due to a fictionalized motion picture and television show of the life of Jesse James, Jr., son of Jesse James, the notorious outlaw of the old West.

In 1924 in Chicago, Illinois, two brilliant, immensely wealthy eighteen-year-old university graduates, Nathan F. Leopold, Jr., and Richard Loeb, intent upon personal pleasure and the need for a "thrill," committed one of the most shocking and senseless crimes ever perpetrated by killing their cousin, Robert Franks, age fourteen. (For a detailed account of the crime, see Chapter 1 of the author's *Society on Trial* [Charles C. Thomas Publisher, 1965] and the author's book review of Leopold's *Life Plus 99 Years* [Doubleday & Co., 1958], appearing in the April 1958 issue of *Columbia Law Review*.) In 1956 the defendant author Meyer Levin, a fellow student with Leopold at the University of Chicago many years previous, published a fictionalized version of the crime in a book, *Compulsion*. The author utilized impressions, thoughts, and ideas as well as imaginary dialogue in establishing motivation for the crime; but this blend of fact and fiction did not disguise the identity of the plaintiff, who had served almost thirty-five years in prison and was only two years away from a probable pardon from the Governor of Illinois. Plaintiff objected vehemently to the book, the subsequent play, and the motion picture advertising his name and likeness, which were appropriated without his consent by the defendant author. In Leopold v. Levin the Illinois trial court upheld the defense on the ground that Leopold was still a public figure, a subject of legitimate public interest; that the novel, play, and motion picture were deemed to be fair comment on a matter of public interest; that freedom of speech and freedom of press were overriding considerations; and that plaintiff had in effect waived any right of privacy by his public activity in 1957 and in 1958 as well as by his writing his own biography, *Life Plus 99 Years*. The trial court had made a preliminary finding for the plaintiff, but Judge Abraham Brussell of the Cook County Circuit Court in early 1968 reversed that ruling by holding in favor of the defendant author of a fictionalized biography (aff 259 NE2d 250, 1970). Among other holdings in favor of the defendant author by Judge Brussell were the following: the fact that publication was for profit was totally irrelevant as to protection of freedom of the press; a fictional novel concerning a voluntary public figure involved in an incident of general public interest should be protected by the First Amendment regardless of its embellishments; there was no claim of intentional or reckless falsity against the author; and the book, play, and motion picture did not outrage any community notions of decency so that the constitutional protection of free expression would be forfeited. However, it should be noted that the author wrote his novel thirty-two years after the crime, and the privacy craved by Leopold upon his release from prison in 1958 simply did not mature. Leopold was again subjected to an attack related and unrelated to his original sin, for which he had dearly paid with thirty-five years of his life in prison.

In Pring v. Penthouse International, Ltd. (695 F2d 438, 10th Cir 1982; cert den 103 S Ct 3112, 1983) plaintiff sued the magazine publisher, claiming that the publication was an invasion of her privacy. The publication described "Charlene," her thoughts as "Miss Wyoming" at the Miss America Pageant in Atlantic City, New Jersey, and depicted her simulating fellatio with her baton during her talent routine. The article also detailed several acts of fellatio that caused men to rise into the air! The plaintiff, who was "Miss Wyoming" when the article was published, claimed that the article about "Charlene" depicted her and placed her in a "false light," and the jury agreed. But the Tenth U.S. Court of Appeals overturned the jury verdict upon the basis that the action was for defamation and there was no separate cause of action in privacy since defamation and privacy involved "the same First Amendment considerations." In effect, the appellate court found a way out of the dilemma since it also found no false statement of fact and wrongly opined that to support a "false light" privacy action there had to be a false statement of fact. The focus of the federal appellate court should have been on whether the published material was "offensive to a reasonable person," regardless of whether the statement was factual or not. The right of the plaintiff to maintain the integrity of her reputation and privacy is an important consideration which the federal appellate court seems to have overlooked in its haste to protect the publication that portrayed an identifiable person in a defamatory context under the guise of fiction. The mere fact that some of the events portrayed in the publication were incredible should not have detracted from the protection of plaintiff's privacy.

Parody is a writing in which language and style of an author or a work are closely imitated for comic effect or ridicule, often with certain peculiarities greatly heightened or exaggerated. In New York parody has been actionable as an appropriation of one's name or likeness under the New York Civil Rights Law (Lombardo v. Doyle, Dane & Birnbach, Inc., 396 NYS2d 661, 1977). Yet parody is one of the oldest forms of literary expression, as illustrated by Hippomax of Ephesus, who in 530 B.C. parodied the *Iliad*, and by Cervantes, who in his *Don Quixote* parodied a Spanish novel on chivalry. Today courts are less willing to protect the parody defense, as is evident in the U.S. Ninth Circuit Court of Appeals decision in Loew's Inc. v. Columbia Broadcasting System (131 F Supp 165, SC Cal 1955; aff. under name of Benny v. Loew's, Inc., 239 F2d 532, 9th Cir 1956). Here it was held that the parody borrowed too heavily from the original work and constituted an infringement of copyright. The point is that the original author's property right, as well as privacy right, was invaded or intruded upon in an unreasonable manner.

2.7 PUBLIC DISCLOSURE OF PRIVATE FACTS

Another form of invasion of privacy is found in the cause of action for publicity of a highly objectionable kind, i.e., giving out to the public private information about the plaintiff, even though the information is true. In Diaz v. Oakland Tribune, Inc. (139 Cal App3d 118, 1983) the plaintiff claimed that defendant newspaper published "highly embarrassing private facts" which caused her to suffer "severe emotional distress." It appears that plaintiff is a transsexual, having been born a male in Puerto Rico in 1942; in 1975, while a resident of California, gender-corrective surgery was performed. According to plaintiff, the surgery was a great success; by all outward appearances she looked and behaved as a woman and was accepted by the public as a woman. She "scrupulously kept the surgery a secret from all but her immediate family and closest friends." In 1978 defendant newspaper printed the following:

> More Education Stuff: The students at the College of Alameda will be surprised to learn their student body president, Toni Diaz, is no lady, but is in fact a man whose real name is Antonio.
>
> Now I realize, that in these times, such a matter is no big deal, but I suspect his female classmates in P. E. 97 may wish to make other showering arrangements.

The jury in a special verdict found that defendants did publicly disclose a private fact concerning the plaintiff, that the fact was private and not public information, that the fact was not newsworthy, that the fact was highly offensive to a reasonable person of ordinary sensibilities, that defendants disclosed the fact with knowledge that it was highly offensive or with reckless disregard of whether it was highly offensive, and that the disclosure proximately caused the injury or damage to the plaintiff. But the California appellate court reversed plaintiff's favorable jury verdict on the basis of an abridgement of "this constitutionally recognized right of free speech and press." The issue of "newsworthiness" also overrode the issue of "public disclosure of private facts," as found by the court, despite the court's evaluation of the evidence:

> Here there is no evidence to suggest that the fact of Diaz's gender-corrective surgery was part of the public record. To the contrary, the evidence reveals that Diaz took affirmative steps to conceal the fact by changing her driver's license, social security, and high school records, and by lawfully changing her name. The police records, upon which Jones relied, contained information concerning one Antonio Diaz. No mention was made of Diaz's new name or gender. In order to draw the connection, Jones relied upon unidentified confidential sources. Under the circumstances we conclude that Diaz's sexual identity was a private matter.
>
> We also do not consider Diaz's Puerto Rican birth to be a public record in this instance. In any event, defendants did not rely on that document and cannot be heard to argue that the information contained therein is public. Moreover, matter which was

once of public record may be protected as private facts where disclosure of that information would not be newsworthy.

The court in analyzing the issue of "newsworthiness" delineated a three-part test, to wit: (1) the social value of the facts published; (2) the depth of the article's intrusion into ostensibly private affairs; and (3) the extent to which the party voluntarily acceded to a position of public notoriety. The court concluded that "the jury was the proper body to answer the question of whether the article was newsworthy or whether it extended beyond the bounds of decency." Thus, the court's reversal on the basis of instructional errors to the jury would enable the defendants in a new trial to assert their defenses of freedom of press and of newsworthiness. However, Comment d to Section 652D of Restatement (Second) of Torts raises an important aspect of the defense by the newspaper, to wit: the public must have a legitimate interest in having the information made available, and that question of fact was left unanswered by the court.

It is self-evident that the law is not for the protection of the hypersensitive, for everyone must to a reasonable extent lead a life exposed to public gaze. Indeed, what is public record is no longer within the zone of privacy, as illustrated by Cox Broadcasting Co. v. Cohn (420 US 469, 1976), where the U.S. Supreme Court opined that the media may disseminate information which is of public record without fear of liability: the rights protected under the First and Fourteenth Amendments are superior to the right of privacy where the information published is already a matter of public record. Here plaintiff's daughter was raped, and a Georgia statute made the publication of a rape victim's name a misdemeanor. At the criminal trial a reporter discovered the name of the rape victim and broadcasted the name over a television station owned by defendant. The court sidestepped the Georgia statute by balancing the interest in freedom of the press against the right of privacy. The court observed that the name of the rape victim was accurately reported and was a matter of public record for any person going to court to ascertain the identity of the rape victim; also, the entire matter was of legitimate public interest, and the defendant television station was only fulfilling its duty to report and inform the public on matters of current news interest. Prior censorship by the Georgia statute was condemned; public figures in a sensational trial for rape and murder have no right to complain of invasions of privacy which reasonably relate to their roles as public figures. It should be noted that Section 652D (b) of Restatement (Second) of Torts requires that the material be "not of legitimate concern to the public" if the right of privacy is to be respected in a case of public disclosure of private facts. If a plaintiff is tried for murder and is acquitted, it is not an invasion of his privacy for newspapers to give reports on his past history and daily life, even if the newspaper reports are published after the trial has ended. However, the newsworthiness of the story must not be stale, as was the case in Cantrell v. Forest City Publishing Co. (supra), which involved embellishment in a "false light" (see §2.4 herein).

The necessity for public disclosure of private facts is another factor to be taken into consideration in evaluating the nature of the right of privacy. In Brents v. Morgan (299 SW 967, 1927) the creditor posted publicly a sign reading: "Dr. W. R. Morgan owes an account here of $49.67. And if promises would pay an account, this account would have been settled long ago. This account will be advertised as long as it remains unpaid." The Kentucky court had no difficulty in finding invasion of the right of privacy because there was no necessity for public disclosure of private facts. On the other hand, in Sipple v. Chronicle Publishing Co. (154 Cal App3d 1040, 1984) it was held that the plaintiff cannot recover for public disclosure of private facts where the defendant merely gave further publicity to matters which the plaintiff had left open to the public eye. "The line is to be drawn when the publicity ceases to be the giving of information to which the public is entitled, and becomes a morbid sensational prying into private lives for its own sake." (The California court quoted freely from Virgil v. Time, Inc., 527 F2d 1122, 9th Cir 1975.) However, a private disclosure to an employer or some other person with a legitimate interest in the subject matter has generally been regarded as permissible, as illustrated by Vogel v. W. T. Grant Co. (327 A2d 133, 1974). Here plaintiffs, credit customers of defendant, alleged that defendant, in order to coerce payment, had contacted third parties and engaged in "a systematic program of harassment." While the lower courts found an invasion of privacy, the Pennsylvania Supreme Court reversed on the ground that defendant's conduct did not "rise to the level of an invasion of privacy." The court found no unreasonable publicity.

> The only persons notified of the arrearage in the Smith account were Smith's employer and mother. While four persons, three relatives and one employer, were contacted in connection with the Vogel account, even notification of this small group does not, in this case, constitute publication. We need not now determine how many outside parties must be notified to make a creditor's disclosures rise to the level of publication. We hold only that in these circumstances notification of two or four third parties is not sufficient to constitute publication. Without proof of publication, appellees have not established an actionable invasion of privacy.

In Biederman's of Springfield v. Wright (322 SW2d 892, Mo 1959) the creditor's agent went to a public restaurant where the debtor worked as a waitress and in a loud voice and degrading manner made demands that she pay her debt. The agent also accused the waitress and her husband of being "dead beats" and of never intending to pay for the merchandise. The Missouri court under these facts held that the oral communication which publicly disclosed private facts constituted an invasion of privacy. But in Voneye v. Turner (240 SW2d 588, 1951) the Kentucky appellate court ruled that a letter written by a creditor to the debtor's employer seeking assistance of the employer in the debt collection did not invade the debtor's right of privacy because the employer had a legitimate interest in the debts of his employee, and furthermore it was customary in Kentucky to refer such deliquencies of employees to employers.

Plaintiff was a contestant on a quiz show produced by defendant broadcasting company; subsequently the quiz show was exposed as a partial fraud in that selected contestants (other than the plaintiff) had been given the answers to questions in advance of the show. Plaintiff, a school teacher, alleged that his reputation had been harmed and that his teaching career was jeopardized by his involvement in the quiz show. The defense moved to dismiss on the ground that the complaint was an amalgam of invasion of privacy, deceit, libel, or slander, and an action for personal injury, and that defendant could not respond properly. The New York court ruled that defendant's conduct was tortious, but dismissed the suit on the basis of the one-year statute of limitations in New York for libel and slander actions. It appeared that the defendant had intentionally misrepresented the honesty of the quiz show both to the contestants and to the public, had acted solely for its own selfish benefit in total disregard of the rights of contestants who had been intentionally tricked into competing, and that, if defendant's activities were exposed, the exposure would cause injury to the reputation and the interests of innocent contestants. The New York Appellate Division in Morrison v. National Broadcasting Co. (24 AD2d 284, 1965) ruled that those contestants injured by defendant's course of conduct should be allowed redress as a ''personal injury'' under a six-year statute of limitations. However, the New York Court of Appeals in 1966 unanimously reversed the appellate court on the ground that the essence of the complaint was ''defamation,'' and that action was still barred by the one-year statute of limitations. It is submitted that the New York Court of Appeals was simply uncomfortable with the fact that the cause of action herein did not fit into a recognized tort category and therefore it was ''bastardized'' as ''defamation,'' which it decidedly was not. In Brueggemeyer v. Associated Press (609 F2d 825, 1980) the Fifth U.S. Court of Appeals affirmed defendant's motion for summary judgment because defendant's reporting of legal proceedings to which the plaintiffs were parties simply did not fall within any of the four categories of the tort of invasion of privacy: ''There was no invasion of privacy in the accurate reporting of a newsworthy event.''

A lawyer's client has a legitimate expectation of privacy, regardless of whether he owns or possesses the files, according to the Ninth U.S. Court of Appeals in DeMassa v. Nunez (770 F2d 1505, 9th Cir 1985). Here the client successfully challenged a file search by the government of the lawyer's office. The court was concerned about public disclosure of private facts, especially since the attorney-client relationship demanded confidentiality. Even the Sixth Amendment on the right to effective assistance of counsel and the Fifth Amendment on protection against discrimination support the client's expectation of privacy. The relationship of attorney and client is spelled out in New York in Section 4503 of the Civil Practice and Law Rules (CPLR):

(a) *Confidential communication privileged; non-judicial proceedings.* Unless the client waives the privilege, an attorney or his employee, or any person who obtains without the knowledge of the client evidence of a confidential communication made between the attorney or his employee and the client in the course of professional employment, shall not disclose, or be allowed to disclose such communication, nor shall the client be compelled to disclose such communication, in any action, disciplinary trial or hearing, or administrative action, proceeding or hearing conducted by or on behalf of any state, municipal or local government agency or by the legislature or any committee or body thereof. Evidence of any such communication obtained by any such person, and evidence resulting therefrom, shall not be disclosed by any state, municipal or local government agency or by the legislature or any committee or body thereof. The relationship of an attorney and client shall exist between a professional service corporation organized under article fifteen of the business corporation law to practice as an attorney and counselor-at-law and the clients to whom it renders legal services.
(b) *Wills.* In any action involving the probate, validity or construction of a will, an attorney or his employee shall be required to disclose information as to the preparation, execution or revocation of any will or other relevant instrument, but he shall not be allowed to disclose any communication privileged under subdivision (a) which would tend to disgrace the memory of the decedent.

The attorney-client privilege applies, according to People v. Belge (399 NYS2d 539, 1977), only if the asserted holder of the privilege is or sought to become a client, the person to whom communication was made is a member of the bar or is acting as an attorney, the communication relates to a fact of which the attorney was informed by his client without the presence of strangers for a purpose of not committing a crime or tort, and the privilege has been claimed and not waived by the client.

Other privileged communications in New York include the spouses (Section 4502 CPLR), to wit: "(b) A husband or wife shall not be required, or, without consent of the other if living, allowed to disclose a confidential communication made by one to the other during marriage"; and the physician, dentist, and nurse (Section 4504 CPLR) have similar privileged communications.

(a) *Confidential information privileged.* Unless the patient waives the privilege, a person authorized to practice medicine, registered professional nursing, licensed practical nursing or dentistry shall not be allowed to disclose any information which he acquired in attending a patient in professional capacity, and which was necessary to enable him to act in that capacity. The relationship of a physician and patient shall exist between a medical corporation, as defined in article forty-four of the public health law, a professional service corporation organized under article fifteen of the business corporation law to practice medicine, and the patients to whom they respectively render professional medical services.

A patient who, for the purpose of obtaining insurance benefits, authorizes the disclosure of any such privileged communication to any person shall not be deemed to have waived the privilege created by this subdivision. For purposes of this subdivision:

1. ''person'' shall mean any individual, insurer or agent thereof, peer review committee, public or private corporation, political subdivision, government agency, department or bureau of the state, municipality, industry, co-partnership, association, firm, trust, estate, or any other legal entity whatsoever, and

2. ''insurance benefits'' shall include payments under a self-insured plan.

(b) *Identification by dentist; crime committed against patient under sixteen.* A dentist shall be required to disclose information necessary for identification of a patient. A physician, dentist or nurse shall be required to disclose information indicating that a patient who is under age of sixteen years has been the victim of a crime.
(c) *Mental or physical condition of deceased patient.* A physician or nurse shall be required to disclose any information as to the mental or physical condition of a deceased patient privileged under subdivision (a), except information which would tend to disgrace the memory of the decedent, either in the absence of an objection by a party to the litigation or when the privilege has been waved:

1. by the personal representative, or the surviving spouse, of the next of kin of the decedent; or

2. in any litigation where the interests of the personal representative are deemed by the trial judge to be adverse to those of the estate of the decedent, by any party in interest; or

3. if the validity of the will of the decedent is in question, by the executor named in the will, or the surviving spouse or any heir-at-law or any of the next of kin or any other party in interest;

the clergy (Section 4505 CPLR), to wit:

Unless the person confessing or confiding waives the privilege, a clergyman, or other minister of any religion or duly accredited Christian Science practitioner, shall not be allowed to disclose a confession or confidence made to him in his professional character as spiritual advisor;

and the psychologist (Section 4507 CPLR), to wit:

The confidential relations and communications between a psychologist registered under the provisions of article one hundred fifty-three of the education law and his client are placed on the same basis as those provided by law between attorney and client, and nothing in such article shall be construed to require any such privileged communications to be disclosed.

A client who, for the purpose of obtaining insurance benefits, authorizes the disclosure of any such privileged communication to any person shall not be deemed to have waived the privilege created by this section. For purposes of this section:

1. ''person'' shall mean any individual, insurer or agent thereof, peer review committee, public or private corporation, political subdivision, government agency, department or bureau of the state, municipality, industry, co-partnership, association, firm, trust, estate or any other legal entity whatsoever; and

2. ''insurance benefits'' shall include payments under a self-insured plan.

2.8 THE PRESS AND THE RIGHT OF PRIVACY

The press, including all media, is a major institution in society, wielding immense power over the right of privacy. The press frequently raises constitutional objections based upon First Amendment rights to defend charges of invasion of the right of privacy. The press has pointed out that the gathering of information is as essential to a free press as the publishing of that information, and that any infringement upon the gathering of information, especially by modern technological methods, infringes upon the First Amendment and freedom of the press. But allowing the press to ''snoop'' indiscriminately in the home or in private files reduces the most important areas of privacy of individuals to a mere nothing. Furthermore, the U.S. Supreme Court in Houchins v. KQED (438 US 1, 1978) has disagreed with the press that the press has greater rights in gathering information than individuals.

In Barber v. Time, Inc. (159 SW2d 291, 1942) the plaintiff suffered from a medical disorder that gave her an insatiable appetite and made her extremely obese. Two photographers took pictures of her in her hospital bed despite her protests, and subsequently the defendant magazine used the photographs to illustrate a news article on obesity. The Missouri court held that the unauthorized action of the press was tortious and that plaintiff-patient in a hospital had a reasonable expectation of freedom from invasion of her privacy. The mere disclosure to the press of a patient's name is not a violation of the patient's right of privacy (Weinberger v. Willuhn, 390 NE2d 945, Ill 1979).

The U.S. Supreme Court in the landmark decision in 1964 in New York Times Co. v. Sullivan (376 US 254) explored the scope of the press' freedom to publish. Here in 1960 the newspaper published a full-page advertisement critical of the manner in which the plaintiff commissioner of police in Birmingham, Alabama, had responded to civil rights demonstrations. Plaintiff claimed that, although the advertisement did not mention him by name, it attributed official misconduct to him by inference. The Alabama trial court instructed the jury that the advertisement was libelous per se, leaving the *New York Times* with no defense other than proving the statement or advertisement was true in all respects. Some of the statements were inaccurate, and plaintiff was awarded $500,000. The Alabama Supreme Court affirmed, and the U.S. Supreme Court reversed on the ground that the First Amendment limited the power of the state of Alabama to award damages in a civil libel action brought by a public official against critics of his official conduct. If the criticism is published without ''actual malice,'' i.e., without knowledge that the statement was false and without reckless disregard of whether or not it was false, then the publication is protected by the constitutional guarantees of freedom of speech and freedom of the press. Therefore, public officials and public figures cannot recover damages even in the presence of factual inaccuracies, unless they prove the existence of actual malice on the part of the press.

Ten years later, in 1974, in Gertz v. Robert Welch, Inc. (418 US 323) the

U.S. Supreme Court, however, ruled that ordinary negligence, not actual malice, was sufficient to support an action for defamation against a media defendant if the plaintiff was not a public figure. Here the defendant published an article purporting to demonstrate that the conviction of a Chicago policeman named Nuccio for murder of a youth named Nelson was a Communist frame-up of which plaintiff was the architect. The article falsely stated that plaintiff had a criminal record and was a member of Communist organizations. In point of fact, plaintiff was a reputable lawyer who represented the Nelson family in civil litigation against Nuccio. The jury rendered a $50,000 verdict in favor of the plaintiff, the appellate court affirmed, and the highest court concurred, pointing out initially that

> [t]he communications media are entitled to act on the assumption that public officials and public figures have voluntarily exposed themselves to increased risk of injury from defamatory falsehoods concerning them. No such assumption is justified with respect to a private individual. He has not accepted public office nor assumed an "influential role in ordering society." . . . He has relinquished no part of his interest in the protection of his own good name, and consequently he has a more compelling call on the courts for redress of injury inflicted by defamatory falsehood. Thus, private individuals are not only more vulnerable to injury than public officials and public figures; they are also more deserving of recovery.

Justice Lewis F. Powell, writing for the court, stressed the fact that plaintiff was not a public figure: "He plainly did not thrust himself into the vortex of this public issue, nor did he engage the public's attention in an attempt to influence its outcome. We are persuaded that the trial court did not err in refusing to characterize petitioner as a public figure for the purpose of this litigation. . . ." The court endorsed liability based upon negligence "even if it took every reasonable precaution to ensure the accuracy of its assertions," provided that the compensation for injury does not include punitive damages "at least when liability is not based on a showing of knowledge of falsity or reckless disregard for the truth." The court also refused to permit "strict liability in tort" to be invoked against the press:

> This approach provides a more equitable boundary between the competing concerns involved here. It recognizes the strength of the legitimate state interest in compensating private individuals for wrongful injury to reputation, yet shields the press and broadcast media from the rigors of strict liability for defamation.

Justice Harry A. Blackmun concurred, opining that

> [b]y removing the spectres of presumed and punitive damages in the absence of *Times* malice, the Court eliminates significant and powerful motives for self-censorship that otherwise are present in the traditional libel action. By so doing, the Court leaves what should prove to be sufficient and adequate breathing space for a vigorous press. What

the Court has done, I believe, will have little, if any, practical effect on the functioning of responsible journalism.

It should be noted that where plaintiff is a public official or a public figure, the "actual malice" standard of New York Times Co. v. Sullivan (supra) must be applied, as indeed it was in Avins v. White (627 F2d 637, 3rd Cir, 1980; cert den 449 US 982, 1980), Woy v. Turner (533 F Supp 102, ND GA, 1981), and Decaralho v. daSilva (414 A2d 806, RI, 1980).

While both the New York Times and the Gertz case (supra) dealt with defamation, the "actual malice" standard was applied to the right of privacy action in Time, Inc. v. Hill (see §1.8 herein), where the magazine published an erroneous account about private individuals involved in an incident of public interest. (The incident formed part of the basis for the novel *The Desperate Hours* about violence against a hostage family.) The U.S. Supreme Court here in 1967 opined that "the constitutional protections for speech and press preclude application of the New York statute [on privacy] to redress false reports of matters of public interest in absence of proof that the defendant published the report with knowledge of its falsity or in reckless disregard of the truth." The court continued:

> The guarantees for speech and press are not the preserve of political expression or comment upon public affairs, essential as those are to healthy government. One need only pick up any newspaper or magazine to comprehend the vast range of published matter which exposes persons to public view, both private citizens and public officials. Exposure of the self to others in varying degrees is a concomitant of life in a civilized community. The risk of this exposure is an essential incident of life in a society which places a primary value on freedom of speech and press. [We] have no doubt that the subject of the *Life* article, the opening of a new play linked to an actual incident, is a matter of public interest. "The line between the informing and the entertaining is too elusive for the protection of [freedom of the press]." Erroneous statement is no less inevitable in such case than in the case of comment upon public affairs, and in both, if innocent or merely negligent, [it] must be protected if the freedoms of expression are to have the "breathing space" that they "need [to] survive. . . . " *Times*. . . . We create a grave risk of serious impairment of the indispensable service of a free press in a free society if we saddle the press with the impossible burdens of verifying to a certainty the facts associated in news articles with a person's name, picture or portrait, particularly as related to non-defamatory matter. Even negligence would be a most elusive standard, especially when the content of the speech itself affords no warning of prospective harm to another through falsity. A negligence test would place on the press the intolerable burden of guessing how a jury might assess the reasonableness of steps taken by it to verify the accuracy of every reference to a name, picture or portrait. . . .

And in Cox Broadcasting Co. v. Cohn (95 S Ct 1029, 1975) the court ruled that a state could not impose a right of privacy liability for public dissemination of the name of a rape victim derived from court documents open to the public. Justice White recalled:

[I]n a society in which each individual has but limited time and resources with which to observe at first hand the operations of his government, he relies necessarily upon the press to bring to him in convenient form the facts of those operations. Great responsibility is accordingly placed upon the news media to report fully and accurately the proceedings of government and official records and documents open to the public are the basic data of governmental operations. Without the information provided by the press most of us and many of our representatives would be unable to vote intelligently or to register opinions on the administration of government generally. With respect to judicial proceedings in particular, the function of the press serves to guarantee the fairness of trials and to bring to bear the beneficial effects of public scrutiny upon the administration of justice.

Appellee has claimed in this litigation that the efforts of the press have infringed his right to privacy by broadcasting to the world the fact that his daughter was a rape victim. The commission of crime, prosecutions resulting from it, and judicial proceedings arising from the prosecutions, however, are without question events of legitimate concern to the public and consequently fall within the responsibility of the press to report the operations of government.

[E]ven the prevailing law of invasion of privacy generally recognizes that the interests in privacy fade when the information involved already appears on the public record. The conclusion is compelling when viewed in terms of the First and Fourteenth Amendments and in light of the public interest in a vigorous press.

A Florida statute required any newspaper that ''assails'' the personal character or official record of a candidate for election to print on the demand of the candidate, free of cost, any reply the candidate may make to the charges, in as conspicuous a place and in the same kind of type, provided that the reply takes up no more space than the charges. In Miami Herald Publishing Co. v. Tornillo (418 US 241, 1974) the U.S. Supreme Court struck down this ''right of reply'' statute because it

fails to clear the barriers of the First Amendment because of its intrusion into the function of editors. . . . A newspaper is more than a passive receptacle or conduit for news, comment, and advertising. The choice of material to go into a newspaper, and the decisions made as to limitations on the size of the paper, and content, and treatment of public issues and public officials—whether fair or unfair—constitutes the exercise of editorial control and judgment. It has yet to be demonstrated how governmental regulation of this crucial process can be exercised consistent with First Amendment guarantees of a free press as they have evolved to this time.

2.9 DEBTOR/CREDITOR AND THE RIGHT OF PRIVACY

Another common relationship which gives rise to invasion of the right of privacy is when the plaintiff is a debtor and the defendant is a creditor. Efforts by a creditor to enforce or collect on a debt may involve harassment that does not rise to the status of intentional infliction of emotional distress, as illustrated by Munley v. ISC Financial House, Inc. (584 P2d 1336, Okla 1978). These efforts by the creditor include the gathering of information or data about the private life of the debtor; investigators frequently overstep bounds of reasonableness and even decency. Credit-collection agencies market information and credit histories of delinquent debtors, and the creditor's use of such information and data may invade the privacy of the debtor.

Frequently the creditor's publication or display of the name and likeness of the debtor and the fact of the debtor's delinquency are litigated, and courts handle such claims generally under the public disclosure tort (see §2.7 herein). How far the creditor can go in putting the plaintiff-debtor in a "bad light" (see §2.3 herein) is open to question. Note Vogel v. W. T. Grant Co. (327 A2d 133, Pa 1974; see §2.7 herein). Generally the issue is whether the disclosure was a publication to the public at large or to so many competitors of the plaintiff that it can be shown that such publication constituted public disclosure. (Note Section 652D, Comment d of Restatement [Second] of Torts.)

Still another standard for judging the creditor's activities is the standard of "offensive to a reasonable person" as delineated herein at §2.1 and §2.6. Undoubtedly the reasonable person standard may find offensive the mere publication of a loan delinquency notice to the public at large; a reasonable person may believe that the publication was an attempt to embarrass or cajole the debtor into payment unfairly, and such publication is simply not sufficient to outweigh the damage to the debtor's reputation and privacy interests. The reasonable man may hold to the belief that the reasonable creditor has alternative means of self-help and access to legal means of redress.

2.10 EMPLOYER/EMPLOYEE AND THE RIGHT OF PRIVACY

Privacy issues also arise in the context of the employer/employee relationship, and the employer has certain obligations with respect to handling the problem of information and data about the employee. In Beaumont v. Brown (257 NW2d 522, 1977) the Michigan court found sufficient evidence of an invasion of an employee's privacy when the employer, the U.S. Department of Labor, wrote a lengthy letter to the Army Reserve requesting confirmation of plaintiff's military schedule as well as information concerning military procedures for reservists, but noting that plaintiff had left his job for a month without approval or notification to his supervisor. The letter described the employee's bad employment record in great detail, to the consternation of the Army Reserve. There was a duty on the part of the employer to retain confidential data regarding the employee, especially in view of the general public disclosure of the contents of the letter. On the other hand, in Rogers v. IBM Corp. (500 F Supp 867, 1980) the federal district court in Pennsylvania observed that the private sector company's investigation of the employee's job performance was limited to discussions with and disclosure to company employees, and therefore there was no invasion of employee's right of privacy.

Drug–testing of employees where there is a reasonable suspicion that the employee is impaired by drugs seems to be upheld on the basis that public interest in railroad safety (where railroad workers objected on the ground of invasion of privacy) outweighed individual privacy. (See *New York Times*, November 27, 1985, at p. D1.) This case Luck v. Southern Pacific Transportation Co. involved a computer programmer for the railroad who was asked by her supervisor (who was carrying a glass bottle) to go down the hall to take a urine test. She refused, and was fired the next day; she sued the railroad, contending that unless the railroad had reason to suspect her of using drugs, it had no right to subject her to drug-testing. The California Superior Court, San Francisco County, found for the defendant employer. According to the *National Law Journal* (April 7, 1986 at page 1) massive drug-screening is being conducted by about one-quarter of the leading industrial companies in the United States with drug tests having been administered to nearly five million persons in 1985. Urine testing can tell an employer a great deal about an employee, to wit: pregnancy, heart-condition, manic-depression, epilepsy, diabetes, or schizophrenia, inter alia. Most courts have ruled that urine-testing as well as blood-testing is a search and seizure issue under the Fourth Amendment. In Patchogue-Medford Conference of Teachers v. Board of Education, the New York Supreme Court, Suffolk County, on June 14, 1985, prohibited the local school board from performing drug-testing of teachers being considered for tenure: "An invasive bodily search may be constitutionally made only when based upon supportable objective facts and pursuant to established administrative standards." Student drug-testing was also deemed an invasion of privacy in the New Jersey Superior Court, Bergen County, Odenheim v. Carlstadt-East Rutherford Regional School District decision, delineated herein at §3.4. In 1985 federal judge Harold D. Victor of Des Moines, Iowa, in McDonnell v. Hunter, reinstated a prison guard who had been fired after refusing to take a urine test: "There is no doubt about it—searches and seizures can yield a wealth of information useful to the searcher. (That is why King George III's men so frequently searched the colonists.) That potential however, does not make a governmental employer's search of an employee a constitutionally reasonable one."

2.11 GOVERNMENT REGULATION OF MEDICAL TREATMENT: PERSONAL AUTONOMY

Medical technology, including even heart transplantation, has in recent years come to dominate the medical profession, and the role of the government has been one of regulating the relatively unchecked diffusion of new diagnostic and treatment modalities. Heart transplantation and other life-saving biotechnological innovations, for example, have come under scrutiny for their violations of the right of "personal autonomy," which is but one aspect of the right of privacy, to wit: "a zone of prima facie autonomy, of presumptive immunity from regulation, in addition to that established by the First Amendment" (74

Columbia L Rev 1410, 1974). This right of "personal autonomy" subsumes (a) decision-making with respect of procreation, sexual relations, dying, medical treatment, etc.; (b) bodily integrity, such as matters of abortion or other intrusions into the human body; (c) control over one's body functions, such as avoidance of mind-altering drugs; and (d) controlling dissemination of information about one's medical treatment. The central theme of this right of "personal autonomy" is the individual's freedom to make personal medical decisions without reference, intrusion, or invasion of one's privacy by government.

However, the right of a patient, for example, to refuse medical treatment is not absolute. In Jacobson v. Commonwealth of Massachusetts (197 US 11, 1905) the U.S. Supreme Court in 1905 ruled that Massachusetts' interest in preventing public epidemics overrode the individual's right to refuse vaccination. In contrast thereto is In the Matter of Quinlan (355 A2d 647, NJ 1976), where the New Jersey court determined that the right to terminate one's life by removal of life-supportive appliances outweighed the state's interest in protecting life. In 1979 the U.S. Supreme Court in Rutherford v. U.S. (442 US 544) faced a number of terminally ill cancer patients who sought to enjoin the federal government from interfering with their access to the product Laetrile. The federal district court responded favorably to their claim by invoking the right of choice of treatment and by granting temporary injunctive relief against enforcement of a Federal Food and Drug Administration ban on the introduction of Laetrile into interstate commerce (438 F Supp 1287, WD Okla 1977; aff 582 F2d 1234, 10th Cir, 1978). But the highest court overturned the ban and expressed its desire to accord the federal government wide latitude in regulating the availability of an unproven drug product (442 US 544, 1979). A federal district court in Oregon in Judkins v. U.S. expressed it in these terms: "The outer limits of the right to privacy have not yet been determined, but I am satisfied that the right asserted here (of a cancer patient to choose Laetrile therapy) does not fall within its perimeter." On the other hand, in Andrews v. Ballard (498 F Supp 1038, SD Tex 1980) the federal district court in Texas ruled that the right to decide to undergo medical treatment was among the fundamental personal rights, and that the Texas Medical Practice Act against acupuncture unconstitutionally interfered with the patient's right of privacy. (Note that the Andrews case focused upon the fact of a "personal decision" and upon an individual's right to his/her own body.) In California in People v. Privitera (74 Cal App3d 936; cert den 444 US 949, 1979) the lower court upheld the right of privacy of patients to use Laetrile and reversed the convictions of physicians and other defendants who had provided the drug product to patients in violation of a California statute. The decision emphasized the right of "personal autonomy" and the patient's fundamental right of privacy under both the California and U.S. constitutions. But the California Supreme Court reversed (591 P2d 919, 1979), holding that the right to choose drugs of unproven efficacy is not encompassed by the right of privacy under either constitution.

It should also be noted that this freedom of choice does not carry with it any constitutional entitlement to the financial resources of the government, which financial resources would be necessary to avail a person of the full range of protected choices. See the abortion cases like Maher v. Roe (432 US 464, 1977) and Harris v. McCrae (448 US 297, 1980) to that effect. Indeed, in Thornburgh v. American College of Obstetricians and Gynecologists and in Diamond v. Charles, both cases being argued on November 5, 1985, before the U.S. Supreme Court, challenges were presented to state statutes limiting and directing abortions and also raising jurisdictional concerns that may obviate the need for the court to modify or even overrule its 1973 landmark decision in Roe v. Wade (410 US 113). In the Thornburgh case the Third U.S. Court of Appeals had found Pennsylvania's Abortion Control Act, which imposed consent and reporting requirements and strictly limited abortions after a fetus had become viable, to be unconstitutional, and therefore that appellate court had enjoined the statute's enforcement (737 F2d 283, 1984). In the Diamond case the Illinois statute on abortion was attacked by physicians who alleged that the statute inhibited their medical judgment and violated ethical responsibilities to patients; the Seventh U.S. Court of Appeals also found certain sections of the Illinois statute unconstitutional (749 F2d 452, 1985).

2.12 GOVERNMENT POLICY ON HOMOSEXUALITY AND CONSENSUAL SEXUAL ACTIVITY

The sexual relations of gay men and lesbian women pose a problem from the viewpoint of the right of privacy because governmental policy takes frequent offense at such private behavior. The armed forces, in particular, have often raised the issue, as illustrated by Dronenburg v. Zech (741 F2d 1388, DC Cir, 1984). Here plaintiff, a twenty-seven-year-old naval petty officer, admitted that he was a homosexual and had repeatedly engaged in homosexual conduct in a barracks on a naval base. He was discharged after a hearing for "misconduct due to homosexual acts" in violation of Navy regulations. He filed suit challenging the Navy's policy of mandatory discharge of homosexuals on the grounds of violation of his constitutionally protected right of privacy and of his right to equal protection of the laws under the Fourteenth Amendment. He contended that the government should not interfere with his personal freedom to control intimate personal decisions regarding his own body except by the least restrictive means available and in the presence of a compelling governmental interest. But the court found no decisions where the right of privacy had been defined broadly enough to include homosexual conduct; the court could only cite decisions in which protection of the right of privacy had been extended to marriage (Loving v. Virginia, 388 US 1, 1967), procreation (Skinner v. Oklahoma, 316 US 535, 1942), contraception (Eisenstadt v. Baird, 405 US 438, 1972), family relationships (Prince v. Massachusetts, 321 US 158, 1944), and child-rearing including education (Pierce v. Society of Sisters, 268 US 510, 1925). The court concluded that it could find "no constitutional right to engage in homosexual conduct and that, as judges, we have no warrant to create one."

The court endorsed the idea that morality can be legislated, and that governments are the proper forums for making moral choices based upon majority view in the community.

State governments have legislated on homosexuality and consensual sexual activity in the form of sodomy statutes, for example. A Virginia statute provides:

> If any person shall carnally know in any manner any brute animal, or carnally know any male or female person by the anus or with the mouth, or voluntarily submit to such carnal knowledge, he or she shall be guilty of a Class 6 felony; provided, that if a parent commits such an act with his or her child, and such child is at least thirteen but less than fifteen years of age at the time of the offense, such parent shall be guilty of a Class 3 felony.

Such criminal statutes (VA Code Section 18.2-361, 1981) attest to society's opposition to extending the right of privacy to protect consensual sexual behavior, but the infrequent enforcement of such statutes also permits the opposite conclusion. See Doe v. Commonwealth's Attorney for Richmond (403 F Supp 1199, ED Va, 1975; aff 425 US 901, 1975). However, in State of New York v. Onofre (415 NE2d 936, NY 1980; cert den 451 US 987, 1981), the New York Court of Appeals found the New York criminal statute on sodomy unconstitutional for prohibiting sexual behavior between consenting, unmarried persons and homosexuals. The basis of the decision was not on the right of privacy grounds, but on the equal protection of the laws. The words of Judge David Bazelon in Norton v. Macy (417 F2d 1161, DC Cir 1969) bear attention:

> The notion that it could be an appropriate function of the federal bureaucracy to enforce the majority's conventional codes of conduct in the private lives of its employees is at war with elementary concepts of liberty, privacy and diversity.

The sanctity of marriage and the recognition of marriage as a fundamental right of privacy pertain only to heterosexual relationships. No court has acknowledged a constitutional right to marry a partner of the same sex (Jones v. Hallahan, 501 SW2d 588, Ky 1973); but a statutory prohibition on marriage between persons of the same sex has been held not to violate the First, Eighth, Ninth, or Fourteenth Amendments (Baker v. Nelson, 191 NW2d 185, Minn, 1971). State statutes like Section 1.01 of the Texas Family Code Annotated explicitly require that marriage applicants be members of the opposite sex. But in New York a fifty-seven-year-old male successfully "adopted" his fifty-year-old male lover in In Re Adoption of Robert Paul P. (471 NE2d 424, 1984), although their "marriage" was not recognized.

But the right of association does serve as a threshold for holding unconstitutional those regulations that discriminate against homosexuals and lesbians, as indicated in Gay Student Services v. Texas A & M University (737 F2d 1317, 5th Cir, 1984). The court held that the university could not bar the existence of a homosexual student group on campus, even though the university has a legitimate interest in prohibiting student activities that are likely to incite violence and disrupt school discipline. To the same effect is Fricke v. Lynch (491 F Supp 381, R.I. 1980), which upheld a homosexual student's right to attend the school prom with his date of the same sex.

Some courts have held that the rights of privacy and "personal autonomy" extend to private sexual conduct between consenting adults, whether heterosexual or homosexual (Baker v. Wade, 553 F Supp 1121, Tex, 1982). But other courts have stopped short of extending the right to all persons regardless of their sexual preferences (Wood v. Davison, 351 F Supp 543, Ga, 1972). In Lovisi v. Slayton (363 F Supp 620, Va, 1973) the plaintiff husband and wife and another person engaged in sexual conduct in their home and photographed the sexual acts. Unfortunately, one of the plaintiffs' children took several of the photographs to school, and the police arrested the plaintiffs. Their convictions were affirmed, even though the court agreed that consenting adults, married or single, have a protected right of privacy in sexual activity, even with the presence of a third party. But that right of privacy was waived when the plaintiffs failed to protect themselves in allowing the photographs to be taken:

> By electing to photograph their sexual relations, thus creating the possibility that the intimacy of their acts would be destroyed by future viewing by others, the Lovisis took upon themselves an especially heavy burden to protect their privacy. They did not meet the burden . . . because of their failure to deny other persons access to the photographs.

And in Paris Adult Theatre v. Slayton (413 US 49, 1973) the U.S. Supreme Court observed that "this privacy right encompasses and protects the personal intimacies of the home, the family, marriage, motherhood, procreation, and child-rearing," but did not protect the commercial exhibition of pornographic films shown in an adults-only public theatre.

2.13 DEATH PENALTY AND THE RIGHT TO DIE

While the Eighth Amendment prohibits cruel and unusual punishment, and while the U.S. Supreme Court has repeatedly upheld the use of capital punishment and the death penalty as not violative of the amendment (Gregg v. Georgia, 428 US 153, 1976), it would appear that the highest court has not considered whether the use of the death penalty abrogated a person's right to life or right to privacy. The Massachusetts Supreme Judicial Court in Commonwealth v. O'Neal (339 NE2d 676, 1975) did invalidate a state statute on capital punishment as violative of the constitutional rights of privacy and of life, although the statute was deemed not to have violated the Eighth Amendment. The U.S. Supreme Court in 1891 in Union Pacific Railway Co. v. Botsford

(141 US 250) took occasion to remark: "No right is held more sacred, or is more carefully guarded . . . than the right of every individual to the possession and control of his own body. . . ." It is submitted that the ultimate deprivation of privacy is the *involuntary* taking of life.

The right to privacy protects the individual's interest in becoming, in being, and in remaining a person. The state has a decided interest in preserving life (Hardin v. State of Tennessee, 216 SW2d 708, Tenn, 1948, and In the Matter of Quinlan, 355 A2d 647, N.J., 1976), and there are laws against attempting or assisting the commission of a suicide because the state favors life. Yet the state takes great pain and effort to formalize the execution ceremony in prisons where capital punishment is imposed; interestingly, when a prisoner on death row becomes mentally incompetent, he is not executed until his mental capacity is restored, for otherwise he would not appreciate the gravity of his crime and punishment (which is then totally immaterial to him). Indeed, in Georgia a prisoner has a right of privacy to starve himself to death (Zant v. Prevatte, 286 SE2d 715, 1982). A court in West Virginia, on the other hand, has observed that for a state to permit an inmate to kill himself based upon this right of privacy was nonsensical especially where the state reserved the right to execute the prisoner (State of West Virginia v. Narick, 292 SE2d 54, 1982). There is a right of privacy to choose death by starvation or to accelerate death by other lawful means, but involuntary killing such as the state execution does not fall within that protected right, according to the court.

The right to preserve life as a component of the right of privacy would take the form of banning the death penalty on the ground that the government shall not kill those who want to live. The U.S. Supreme Court in Furman v. Georgia (408 US 238, 1972) struck down the death penalty under the Eighth Amendment on the ground of arbitrariness due to lack of standards to guide juries in deciding on punishment. In Gregg v. Georgia (supra) the court concluded that the form of punishment is not cruel or unusual under the Eighth Amendment if it is not offensive to contemporary community values: "It requires . . . that we look to objective indicia that reflect the public attitude toward a given sanction." It has been argued that while the right to life is fundamental, the death penalty is justified on grounds of deterrence, incapacitation, and retribution. Yet the U.S. Supreme Court in the Gregg case was unconvinced in 1976 that the death penalty deterred crime, incapacitated the offender, or resulted in retribution.

Courts have deemed the right to die voluntarily a component of the right to privacy, particularly in cases involving prisoners on death row. This right to die outside of prison cells often takes the form of euthanasia and has been treated as a form of murder. See 22 *William & Mary L Rev* 327 (1981). However, some courts, like the New Jersey Superior Court in In Re Conroy (486 A2d 1209, 1985), have held that a competent patient has the right to decline any medical treatment including feedings, and furthermore retains that right to die when and if he becomes incompetent. See 16 *Akron L Rev* 162 (1982).

Patients subject to pleas of euthanasia can be incompetent individuals facing certain death (In Re Eichner, 423 NYS2d 580, 1979, where the person was in a coma with no hope of returning to a cognitive sapient life); competent individuals who are terminally ill (Lane v. Candura, 376 NE2d 1232, Mass., 1976, where patient refused to submit to surgical amputation of gangrenous leg); or physically healthy and competent individuals who have simply decided to die rather than face an unpleasant future (State of West Virginia v. Narick, supra; here prisoner fasted to his death).

2.14 RAPE VICTIM IDENTIFICATION

Too frequently the media have utilized their First Amendment right to disclose the identity of a sexual assault or rape victim to the great consternation, pain, suffering, and loss of dignity of the victim. Court records which are in the public domain make the publication of the identity of a child rape victim, for example, not actionable, as shown in Hubbard v. Journal Publishing Co. (368 P2d 147, NM, 1962). And yet there is no social value in disclosing the rape victim's identity, as illustrated by Doe v. Sarasota-Bradenton Florida Television Co. (436 So 2d 328, Fla, 1983). It is readily apparent that the disclosure causes the victim grievous suffering, irreparable harm in some cases, and constitutes an invasion of right of privacy. Unfortunately, the Constitution does not mandate media responsibility or sensitivity for the feelings of others (Rawlings v. Hutchinson Publishing Co., 543 P2d 988, Kan, 1975). As long as the disclosure is truthful and reasonably accurate, there is apparently no breach of privacy (Roshto v. Hebert, 439 So2d 428, La, 1983).

But there are state statutes that prohibit publication of a rape victim's name, as in Napier v. Jefferson Standard Life Insurance Co. (322 F2d 502, 4th Cir, 1963). Rape victims have sued successfully where the fact of rape was a private fact, as in Forsher v. Bugliosi (608 P2d 716, Cal, 1980), or where the hospital acted negligently in making public disclosure of the rape (Griffith v. Rancocas Valley Hospital, decided by the New Jersey Superior Court in 1982). But where the fact of rape is a matter of public record or was taken from a judicial proceeding open to the public, no recourse is left for the victim (Cox Broadcasting Co. v. Cohn, 420 US 469, 1975). There is a presumption even of newsworthiness giving rise to protection under the First Amendment, not for the rape victim but for the media or press. One exception to that axiom appears in Hyde v. City of Columbia (637 SW2d 251, Mo 1982; cert den 459 US 1226, 1983), where the press acted irresponsibly in reporting a crime involving a woman who had reported to the police that she had been abducted at gunpoint. The defendant newspaper printed the story based on the facts in the police record. The assailant thereupon harassed the victim, and she communicated with the newspaper about her predicament. The Missouri appellate court held that disclosure of her name placed here in a "clear and present" danger situation, so that the right to publish the story was qualified by a concomitant duty to protect a citizen's security. Thus, the newspaper was negligent in disclosing a private fact, to wit, the victim's identity.

3

Constitutional Protection of Interests in Personality

3.1 THE CONSTITUTION AND THE RIGHT OF PRIVACY GENERALLY

In the landmark abortion case of Roe v. Wade (410 US 113, 1973) Justice Harry A. Blackmun opined:

> The Constitution does not explicitly mention any right of privacy. In a line of decisions, however, . . . the Court has recognized that a right of personal privacy, or a guarantee of certain areas or zones of privacy, does exist under the Constitution. In varying contexts, the Court or individual Justices have, indeed, found at least the roots of that right in the First Amendment, . . . in the Fourth and Fifth Amendments, . . . in the penumbras of the Bill of Rights, . . . in the Ninth Amendment, . . . or in the concept of liberty guaranteed by the first section of the Fourteenth Amendment . . . These decisions make it clear that only personal rights that can be deemed ''fundamental'' or ''implicit in the concept of ordered liberty'' . . . are included in this guarantee of personal privacy. (P. 152)

It is therefore a legitimate question, Why did not those august persons who wrote the Declaration of Independence, the Constitution, and the Bill of Rights expressly recognize a right of privacy? The answer would appear to be that in the course of the American Revolution the framers of the above documents had other more important concerns than the right of the individual to be let alone. However, the Fourth Amendment did solemnly state: ''The right of the people to be secure in their persons, houses, papers and effects against unreasonable searches and seizures, shall not be violated, and no Warrants shall issue, but upon probable cause, supported by Oath or affirmation, and particularly describing the place to be searched and the person or things to be seized.'' The Americans of 1790 were undoubtedly more concerned with preventing a recurrence of the days of George III than they were of the need to protect the privacy of the indivdiual. Yet the Fourth Amendment clearly defines a segment of privacy, to wit: protection from police invasion of privacy.

The U.S. Supreme Court has recognized that ''a right of personal privacy or a guarantee of certain areas and zones of privacy does exist under the Constitution,'' according to Griswold v. Connecticut (381 US 479, 1965). Here the plaintiff was the director of the Planned Parenthood League, and in that capacity he gave out information, instruction, and medical advice to married persons regarding the use of contraceptives. Connecticut law forbade such activity and also prohibited married couples from using conntraceptive devices. After plaintiff was arrested and convicted for violating the state law, he appealed all the way to the U.S. Supreme Court. Justice William O. Douglas, writing for the majority of the court, delineated the existence of a constitutionally protected right to privacy in the initimate relationship between husband and wife, lying safely within the ''penumbras'' which breathe life and substance into constitutional entitlements, the ''zone of privacy.'' (The Connecticut statute which impinged upon this right of privacy was therefore unconstitutional.) The dissenting opinion of Justice Hugo L. Black found no such right of privacy in the Constitution and poignantly summarized: ''I like my privacy as well as the next one, but I am nevertheless compelled to admit that government has a right to invade it unless prohibited by some specific constitutional provision.''

Another contraceptive case arose before the highest court in 1972 in Eisenstadt v. Baird (405 US 438), and here the Massachusetts statute was also found to be constitutionally wanting:

> It is true that in *Griswold* the right to privacy in question inhered in the marital relationship. Yet the marital couple is not an independent entity with a mind and heart of its own, but an association of two individuals each with a separate intellectual and emotional makeup. If the right of privacy means anything, it is the right of the individual, married or single, to be free from unwarranted governmental intrusion into matters so fundamentally affecting a person as the decision whether to bear or beget a child.

And in 1973 in Roe v. Wade (supra) the court found that the right of privacy was broad enough to encompass a woman's decision whether or not to have an abortion, provided that her decision involved a non-viable fetus and was made in consultation with a licensed physician. These personal choices in contraception and abortion which gave rise to rights of privacy, however, were dealt somewhat of a mortal blow in 1976 when the U.S. Supreme Court affirmed the decision of the federal district court in Virginia in Doe v. Commonwealth's Attorney for Richmond (425 US 901, aff'g 403 F Supp 1199) that denied constitutional protection to choices by homosexuals to have sexual intercourse with consenting adults in private. However, the New Jersey Supreme Court in In the Matter of Quinlan (355 A2d 657, 1976) declared that the constitutional right of privacy was ''broad enough to encompass a patient's decision to decline medical treatment under certain circumstances, in much the same way as it is broad enough to encompass a woman's decision to terminate pregnancy under certain conditions.''

Court decisions have demonstrated that the right of privacy exists under the First Amendment (Stanley v. Georgia, 394 US 557, 1969), under the Ninth Amendment (Griswold v. Connecticut, supra), and under the Due Process of Law clauses of the Fifth and Fourteenth Amendments (Roe v. Wade, supra). But this right of privacy is precisely an individual right of freedom from govenmental intrusion or governmental interference. It is self-evident in the Third Amendment, which protects the individual from the government quartering soldiers in a person's house in time of peace without the consent of the owner of the house; in the Sixth Amendment, which requires that an individual be informed of evidence brought against him in respect of criminal allegations; in the Fifth Amendment, which gives the individual the right not to be compelled to be a witness against himself; in the Ninth Amendment, which guarantees that citizens have many rights, not all of which are defined in the Constitution; in the Tenth Amendment, which reserves individual rights to the people which are not otherwise prohibited by law; and in the Fourteenth Amendment, which guarantees each individual due process of law against intrusion or injury and equal protection of the laws. It can certainly be argued that the catalyst for the American Revolution was the disrespect for privacy rights by George III, but the framers of the constitutional documents did not spell out the parameters of that right of privacy.

This ''constitutional'' right of privacy reflects the fact that there has been much tension between what might be described as a ''private right of privacy,'' i.e., intrusion or interference from non-governmental sources, and a ''public right of privacy,'' i.e., intrusion or interference from govenmental sources. Substantive due process requires that individual liberty be primary, and that government must always justify its actions or inactions and thereby prove itself. Professor Louis Henkin in 74 *Columbia Law Review* 1410 at page 1429 wrote:

> The freedom of speech, press and religion required extraordinary judicial protection against invasions even for the public good, because of their place at the foundation of democracy and because of the unreliability of the political process in regard to them. If other rights—those to be described as within the Right of Privacy—are also to be specially guarded against the democratic political process, similar or other justifications must be found—if there are any. Perhaps unusual respect for autonomy and idiosyncrasy as regards some ''personal'' matters is intuitively felt by all of us, including Justices: that such deference is ''self-evident'' is not self-evident.

3.2 RIGHT OF PRIVACY IN THE CONSTITUTIONAL SETTING

The ''constitutional'' right of privacy is not absolute, for government can properly compel vaccinations (Jacobson v. Massachusetts, 197 US 1, 1905), premarital blood tests, and sterilization of mental defectives (Buck v. Bell, 274

US 200, 1927), for example, and even sanction music in public places for general entertainment in disregard of the individual's private right to enjoy silence (Public Utility Commission v. Pollak, 343 US 451, 1952). In Griswold v. Connecticut (supra) a Connecticut statute forbidding the use of contraceptives, as applied to a married couple, was invalidated on the ground that the statute violated a "constitutional" right of marital privacy. Mr. Justice Douglas emphasized that a "zone of privacy" is created by several fundmental constitutional guarantees, as "specific guarantees in the Bill of Rights have penumbras, formed by emanations from those guarantees that help give them life and substance." He observed that the right of privacy was "older than the Bill of Rights, older than our political parties, older than our school system." Four years later, in 1969, in Stanley v. Georgia (supra) the U.S. Supreme Court declared that it was "fundamental . . . to be free, except in very limited circumstances from unwanted governmental intrusions into one's privacy." And in 1972 in Eisenstadt v. Baird (405 US 438) the court stated: "If the right of privacy means anything, it is the right of the individual, married or single, to be free from unwarranted governmental intrusion into matters so funamentally affecting a person as the decision whether to bear or beget a child." The next year in Roe v. Wade (supra) the court felt that a woman has a "fundamental right of privacy under the Constitution to determine whether or not to terminate her pregnancy," although that right of privacy could be overridden only by a "compelling" state interest. The right of privacy was "founded in the Fourteenth Amendment's concept of personal liberty and restrictions upon State action." In 1983 in City of Akron v. Akron Center for Reproductive Health (462 US 416) the court held unconstitutional certain provisions of the city's abortion ordinance as an unconstitutional interference with a woman's privacy right.

But in Time, Inc. v. Hill (385 US 374, 1967) the highest court ruled that "the constitutional protections for speech and press precluded the application of the New York statute to redress false reports of matters of public interest in the absence of proof that the defendant published the report with knowledge of its falsity or in reckless disregard of the truth." In his concurring opinion Mr. Justice Douglas remarked:

> It seems to me irrelevant to talk of any right of privacy in this context. Here a private person is catapulted into the news by events over which he had no control. He and his activities are then in the public domain. . . . Such privacy as a person normally has ceases when his life has ceased to be private.

Here the First Amendment restricted the operation of the right of privacy more effectively than the New York statute.

In another New York case, New York State Club Association, Inc. v. City of New York, decision dated October 31, 1985, the constitutionality of a city law barring private clubs from discriminating against women and minorities was challenged, inter alia, on the grounds of invasion of privacy. The court, in rejecting the challenge, asserted that "the Constitution does not explicitly mention any right of privacy (Carey v. Population Services International, 431 US 678):

> The Supreme Court, however, has recognized that one aspect of the "liberty" protected by the Due Process Clause of the Fourteenth Amendment is a "right of personal privacy." (Roe v. Wade, 410 US 113, 132.) The right of privacy does entail the right to make decisions concerning "highly personal relationships without undue government intrusion." (Zabloski v. Redhail, 434 US 374, 385–386.) The personal affiliations that exemplify the relationship that are contemplated within the constitutional zone of privacy are those attendant to the creation and sustenance of the family (Roberts v. United States Jaycees, 104 S. Ct 3244, 3250) and cases cited therein. Family relationships, as noted in *Roberts*, "by their nature, involve deep attachments and commitments to the necessarily few other individuals with whom one shares not only a special community of thoughts, experiences and beliefs, but also distinctively personal aspect of one's life. . . . " Such relationships are characterized by relative smallness of the group, a high degree of selectivity to begin and maintain affiliation and seclusion from other critical aspects of the relationship.

The court then pointed out:

> The clubs affected by this legislation must have a membership of over 400 individuals. Such number is not small, nor can it be viewed as exclusive (see Roberts v. United States Jaycess, supra). Moreover, the statute requires that the clubs receive revenues from nonmembers for the conduct of a trade or business. This commercial activity generating revenue from outsiders further undermines the claim of exclusivity. When intimate relationships, such as family and marriage, are involved, the constitutional right to privacy is implicated and these matters may only be regulated when the state demonstrates compelling subordinating interest that cannot be satisfied by less obtrusive means (Carey v. Population Services International, supra). The clubs at which the statute is aimed are not the type of institutions contemplated for protection under the penumbra of privacy envisioned by the Supreme Court. They lack the degree of intimacy normally associated with such rights. Thus, the test is whether the regulated conduct is reasonably related to a legitimate state interest (Village of Belle Terre v. Borass, 416 US 1.) The City's interest in protecting its citizenry from the serious social and personal harms resulting from invidious discrimination is not merely legitimate, it is compelling (Roberts v. United States Jaycees, supra). Discrimination based on archaic and overbroad assumptions and stereotypes about the relative needs and capacities of certain groups deprives persons of their individual dignity and denies society the benefits of wide participation in political, economic and cultural life (Heckler v. Matthews, 104 S. Ct. 1387, 1393).

The "zone of privacy" thus embraces what might be called the "personal autonomy interests" relating to matters of marriage, procreation, contraception, abortion, family relationships, child-rearing, education, and private club membership. See generally Whalen v. Roe (429 US 589, 1977), Paul v. Davis (424 US 693, 1976), and Roe v. Wade (supra).

Still another aspect of the right of privacy in a constitutional setting is found in Nixon v. Administrator of General Services (433 US 425, 1977). The court upheld the constitutionality of the Presidential Recordings and Materials Preservation Act against the privacy interests of the former President, which were outweighed by the great public interest in the documents and recordings, by former President Nixon's status as a public figure, and by the protection within the act against complete disclosure.

3.3 FIRST AMENDMENT AND THE RIGHT OF PRIVACY

The First Amendment to the U.S. Constitution provides in part that "Congress shall make no law . . . abridging the freedom of speech or of the press. . . . " However, these words of "speech" and "press" are not in conflict with the right of privacy, nor is privacy jeopardized by the concepts of "freedom of speech or of the press." In Lloyd Corp. v. Tanner (407 US 551) Justice Lewis F. Powell of the U.S. Supreme Court observed that "the framers . . . did not think these fundamental rights of a free society are incompatible with each other." Indeed, the essence of these freedoms is that a right of privacy is created against governmental intrusion and governmental interference. Justice Douglas in his concurring opinion in Roe v. Wade (supra) stressed that it was the First Amendment which protected the right of privacy concerned with "autonomous control over the development and expression of one's intellect, interests, tastes and personality."

In 1969 in Stanley v. Georgia (394 US 557) the highest court examined the problem of police entering plaintiff's home under a search warrant, seeking evidence of bookmaking activities; the police found and seized three reels of obscene film, and plaintiff was convicted for "knowingly having possession of obscene matter" in violation of Georgia law. Plaintiff's contention that the Georgia statute was unconstitutional was upheld on the basis of the Fourteenth and the First Amendments: "It is now well established that the Constitution protects the right to receive information and ideas. . . . This right to receive information and ideas, regardless of their social worth. . . . is fundamental to our free society . . . also fundamental is the right to be free, except in very limited circumstances, from unwanted governmental intrusions into one's privacy." Justice Thurgood Marshall then opined:

> Whatever may be the justifications for other statutes regulating obscenity, we do not think they reach into the privacy of one's own home. If the First Amendment means anything, it means that a State has no business telling a man, sitting alone in his own house, what books he may read or what films he may watch. Our whole constitutional heritage rebels at the thought of giving government the power to control men's minds.

The asserted right of the state of Georgia "to control the moral content of a person's thought" is "wholly inconsistent with the philosophy of the First Amendment." A note writer in 81 *Yale Law Journal* 309 (1971) at pages 328–329 summed up the holding of the case in these terms:

> The right to read or observe what one pleases necessarily implies the right to receive, and therefore to possess, all constitutionally protected materials. [If] an individual is deterred from acquiring and possessing a non-obscene book because he fears that it may be obscene and that he will be punished for its possession, his right to "read or observe what he pleases" has clearly been "inhibited." The First Amendment will not tolerate any law which causes a man returning home from his local bookstore to wonder whether his latest purchase may lead to his arrest. . . . The individual [must] be allowed to read or observe obscene material in private in order to safeguard his First Amendment rights to read or observe non-obscene material.

But the publication of obscene matter is not guaranteed under the First Amendment (Roth v. U.S., 354 US 476, 1976); nor is public speech, no matter how inflammatory, protected with absolute immunity from legal restrictions (Schenck v. U.S., 249 US 47, 1919). The right of privacy may be said to serve as a counterweight to the First Amendment in the sense that people wronged by invasions of privacy should not be denied relief simply because of the right to freedom of speech and of the press. The California Supreme Court decision in Briscoe v. Reader's Digest Association (4 Cal 3d 529, 1971) recognized this dichotomy in ruling that the publication of plaintiff's name was not newsworthy some eleven years after the crime; the publication was deemed to interfere with plaintiff's rehabilitative process or his right of privacy.

3.4 FOURTH AMENDMENT AND THE RIGHT OF PRIVACY

Under the Fourth Amendment the "people" are given "the right . . . to be secure in their persons, houses, papers, and effects, against unreasonable searches and seizures." Courts have construed this language as having the primary purpose of preventing "unlawful invasion of the sanctity of the home" (Adams v. New York, 192 US 585, 1904) and of insuring "the right of man to retreat into his own home and there be free from unreasonable governmental intrusion" (Silverman v. U.S. 365 US 505, 1961). Justice Louis D. Brandeis in his famous dissent in Olmstead v. U.S. (277 US 438, 1928) saw the Fourth Amendment as the protection for the right of privacy:

> The makers of our Constitution undertook to secure conditions favorable to the pursuit of happiness. They recognized the significance of man's spiritual nature, of his feelings and of his intellect. They knew that only a part of the pain, pleasure and satisfactions of life are to be found in material things. They sought to protect Americans in their

> beliefs, their thoughts, their emotions and their sensations. They conferred, as against the government, the right to be let alone—the most comprehensive of rights and the right most valued by civilized man. To protect that right every unjustifiable intrusion by the government upon the privacy of the individual, whatsoever the means employed, must be deemed a violation of the Fourth Amendment.

The dissent of Justice Hugo Black in Griswold v. Connecticut (supra) took a dim view of the right of privacy under the Fourth Amendment, pointing out that

> There are guarantees in certain specific constitutional provisions which are designed in part to protect privacy at certain times and places with respect to certain activities. [But] I think it belittles [the Fourth] Amendment to talk about it as though it protects nothing but "privacy." [The] average man would very likely not have his feelings soothed any more by having his property seized openly than by having it seized privately and by stealth. [And] a person can be just as much, if not more, irritated, annoyed and injured by an unceremonious public arrest by a policeman as he is by a seizure in the privacy of his office or home.

However, three years later, in 1967, in Katz v. U.S. (389 US 347) the U.S. Supreme Court relied upon an expectation of privacy. Here the criminal defendant challenged his conviction based on evidence obtained by unwarranted electronic eavesdropping on conversations conducted from a public telephone booth. In reversing the conviction the court declared:

> [T]he Fourth Amendment protects people, not places. What a person knowingly exposes to the public, even in his own home or office, is not a subject of Fourth Amendment protection. . . . But what he seeks to preserve as private, even in an area accessible to the public, may be constitutionally protected. . . .
>
> . . . What [the defendant] sought to exclude when he entered the booth was not the intruding eye—it was the uninvited ear. . . . One who occupies [a telephone booth], shuts the door behind him, and pays the toll that permits him to place a call is surely entitled to assume that the words he utters into the mouthpiece will not be broadcast to the world. To read the Constitution more narrowly is to ignore the vital role that the public telephone has come to play in private communications.

Thus, the court extended a hand to the criminal defendant who was deprived of his privacy by official action. In Menard v. Mitchell (328 F Supp 718, DC Cir, 1971) the court summed up the restraints necessary to curb governmental abuse of its data-gathering powers which offend the individual's rights of privacy:

> A heavy burden is placed on all branches of Government to maintain a proper equilibrium between the acquisition of information and the necessity to safeguard privacy. Systematic recordation and dissemination of information about individual citizens is a form of surveillance and control which may easily inhibit freedom. . . . If information available to Government is misused to publicize past incidents in the lives of its citizens

> the pressure for conformity will be irresistible. Initiative and individuality can be suffocated and a resulting dullness of mind and conduct will become the norm. . . . In short, the overwhelming power of the Federal Government to expose [citizens' lives to public scrutiny] must be held in proper check.

The interest of government in collecting information about a person's sex life (Shuman v. City of Philadelphia, 470 F Supp 449, ED Pa, 1979) or about lawful First Amendment activities engaged in by individuals and groups (Alliance to End Repression v. City of Chicago, 561 F Supp 537, ND Ill, 1982), for example, without a showing of some important and legitimate government interest, clearly runs counter to the proper role of government in a democratic society.

The Fourth Amendment by its application to the right of privacy has produced a variety of situations that are not readily distinguishable on their peculiar facts. In Florida Medical Assn. v. Department of Health, Education and Welfare (479 F Supp 1291, Fla, 1979) a physician's privacy interest was held to outweigh the public's interest in knowing the amounts of public monies paid to him in the form of Medicare reimbursements. In Harbolt v. Department of State (616 F2d 772, 5th Cir, 1980) the disclosure of the names and addresses of U.S. citizens imprisoned abroad was held to constitute an unwarranted invasion of their privacy. The Fifth U.S. Court of Appeals held that disclosure would not further the public interest, even though such information would be of value in evaluating the exercise of the defendant's duties regarding foreign prisoners. The court determined that "great embarrassment" would be caused the prisoners, their families and their friends by the disclosure, and "great embarrassment" was tantamount to an invasion of privacy. On the other hand, an official ruling of the Attorney General of Kentucky (Ky Op Atty Gen 77-394, 1977) demonstrates how ridiculous the unwarranted expansion of the concept of privacy can be; here the Kentucky Open Records Law (Ky Rev Stat Sec. 61.870–61, 884, 1980) contained an exemption for personal information, the disclosure of which would constitute a clearly unwarranted invasion of personal privacy. A University professor asked for records pertaining to her evaluation, and the University refused to comply; the Kentucky Attorney General supported the university position: "Since the public is not entitled to inspect the teacher's evaluation, the teacher has no more right than the public to inspect the evaluation. . . . "

In New York a defendant was arrested after police seized a bag of drugs he left in a store; the police contended that defendant had voluntarily abandoned the bag, thereby waiving his constitutional right against illegal searches and seizures. The New York Supreme Court, New York County, in People v. Bagley in December 1985, denied the defendant's motion to suppress the confiscated drugs, concluding that defendant had indeed "ditched" the drugs when he was observed by plainclothes policemen. At the same time the defendant also abandoned "any reasonable expectation of privacy he may have had."

The right of privacy issue arose in a New Jersey case, Odenheim v. Carlstadt-East Rutherford Regional School District, decided by the New Jersey Superior Court in Hackensack on December 9, 1985. Here the court ruled that a public school cannot force its students to undergo urine testing for drugs as part of the annual school physical examinations for students. To do so would violate the students' Fourth Amendment right as well as their "legitimate expectation of privacy and personal security." The defendant school board argued that the primary purpose of the urinalysis was to detect "any physical defects, illnesses or communicable diseases," and the student who tests positively for drugs is not subject to any civil or criminal sanctions. The defense also stressed that no "individual suspicion" was required because all students had to undergo the drug-testing, and furthermore there was no discretion on the part of school officials. But the court, relying upon the U.S. Suprme Court decision in State of New Jersey v. T.L.O. (105 S Ct 733, 1985), found the school board policy to be unconstitutional, and did not accept the defense contention that the drug-testing was a medical examination.

> [The policy] violates the reasonable privacy expectations of school children. The defendants' activities are not reasonably related in scope to the circumstances which initially justified the interference. School policy already provides for exclusion and/or suspension of students who are involved with drug activity. . . . Defendants' policy is an attempt to control student discipline under the guise of a medical procedure, thereby circumventing strict due process requirements.

Warrantless aerial surveillance of a backyard to detect possible criminal activity by the homeowners was enjoined by the California Supreme Court in State of California v. Cook (710 P2d 299, 1985) as violative of the search and seizure provision of the California Constitution. Based upon the surveillance, the police found marijuana and after a search warrant was issued the banned substance was seized. In reversing the conviction the court opined: "While the skies are accessible to the public—and even though private air traffic may regularly wing over one's property—simply because one may have to put up with the occasional downward glance of a passing pilot or passenger, does not abrogate the force of one's demand that police officers . . . refrain from examining the air details of one's backyard."

3.5 OTHER AMENDMENTS AND THE RIGHT OF PRIVACY

The Ninth Amendment, which dilineates the fact that "the enumeration in the Constitution, of certain rights, shall not be construed to deny or disparage others retained by the people," has also been cited in support of the right of privacy. Justice Arthur J. Goldberg in his concurring opinion in Griswold v. Connecticut (supra) declared:

While this Court has had little occasion to interpret the Ninth Amendment (citing United Public Workers v. Mitchell, 330 US 75, 94–95, 67 S.Ct 556, 556–567, 91 L.Ed 754; Tennessee Electric Power Co. v. TVA, 306 US 118, 143–144, 59 S.Ct. 366, 372, 83 L.Ed. 543; and Ashwander v. TVA, 297 US 288, 330–331, 56 S.Ct. 466, 475466, 475, 80 L.Ed. 688. See also Calder v. Bull, 3 Dall. 386, 388, 1 L.Ed. 648; Loan Assn. v. Topeka, 20 Wall. 655 662–663, 22 L.Ed. 455) it cannot be presumed that any clause in the constitution is intended to be without effect. . . . To hold that a right so basic and fundamental and so deep-rooted in our society as the right of privacy in marriage may be infringed because that right is not guaranteed in so many words by the first eight amendments to the Constitution is to ignore the Ninth Amendment and to give it no effect whatsoever. . . . I do not mean to imply that the Ninth Amendment is applied against the States by the Fourteenth [nor] to state that the Ninth Amendment constitutes an independent source of rights protected from infringment by either the States or the Federal Government. Rather, the Ninth Amendment shows a belief of the Constitution's authors that fundamental rights exist that are not expressly enumerated in the first eight amendments and an intent that the list of rights included there not be deemed exhaustive . . . this court has held, often unanimously, that the Fifth and Fourteenth Amendments protect certain fundamental personal liberties from abridgement by the Federal Government or the States. [I] do not see how this [interpretation of the Ninth Amendment] broadens the authority of the Court; rather it serves to support what this Court has been doing in protecting fundamental rights.

[While] the Ninth Amendment—and indeed the entire Bill of Rights—originally concerned restrictions upon federal power, the subsequently enacted Fourteenth Amendment prohibits the States as well from abridging fundamental personal liberties. [In] sum, the Ninth Amendment simply lends strong support to the view that the "liberty" protected by the Fifth and Fourteenth Amendments from infringement by the Federal Government or the States is not restricted to rights specifically mentioned in the first eight amendments.

Professor Patterson in his *The Forgotten Ninth Amendment* (1955) urged that the Ninth Amendment be used to protect unspecified "natural and inalienable rights" (p. 4). Justice Hugo Black's dissent in Griswold v. Connecticut (supra) pointed out that

the whole history [shows] that the Ninth Amendment was intended to protect against the idea that "by enumerating particular exceptions to the grant of power to the Federal Government, those rights which were not singled out, were intended to be assigned into the hands of the General Government (the United States) and were consequently insecure." That Amendment was passed [to] limit the Federal Government to the powers granted expressly or by necessary implication. [This] fact is perhaps responsible for the peculiar phenomenon that for a period of a century and a half no serious suggestion was ever made that the Ninth Amendment, enacted to protect state powers against federal invasion, could be used as a weapon of federal power to prevent state legislatures from passing laws they consider appropriate to govern local affairs.

The Fourteenth Amendment, Section 1, mandates that "no State shall make or enforce any law which shall abridge the privileges or immunities of citizens

. . . nor shall any State deprive any person of life, liberty or property, without due process of law; nor deny to any person within its jurisdiction the equal protection of the laws.'' In Skinner v. Oklahoma (315 US 535, 1942) an Oklahoma statute authorized the sterilization of persons convicted more than twice of ''felonies involving moral turpitude.'' The U.S. Supreme Court declared the statute unconstitutional as in violation of the equal protection provisions of the Fourteenth Amendment. Justice William O. Douglas, writing for the court, expounded:

We are dealing here with legislation which involves one of the basic civil rights of man. Marriage and procreation are fundamental to the very existence and survival of the race. The power to sterilize, if exercised, may have subtle, far-reaching and devastating effects. In evil or reckless hands it can cause races or types which are inimical to the dominant group to wither and disappear. There is no redemption for the individual whom the law touches. [We] mention these matters [in] emphasis of our view that strict scrutiny of the classification which a State makes in a sterilization law is essential, lest unwittingly or otherwise invidious discriminations are made. . . . When the law lays an unequal hand on those who have committed intrinsically the same quality of offense and sterilizes one and not the other, it has made as an invidious a discrimination as if it had selected a particular race or nationality for oppressive treatment.

The concurring opinion of Justice Hugo Black in Griswold v. Connecticut (supra) referred to the Fourteenth Amendment in these words:

In my view, the proper constitutional inquiry in this case is whether this Connecticut statute infringes the Due Process Clause of the Fourteenth Amendment because the enactment violates basic values ''implicit in the concept of ordered liberty.''. . . . I believe that it does. While the relevant inquiry may be aided by resort to one or more of the provisions of the Bill of Rights, it is not dependent on them or any of their radiations. The Due Process Clause of the Fourteenth Amendment stands, in my opinion, on its own bottom. . . .

While I could not more heartily agree that judicial ''self restraint'' is an indispensable ingredient of sound constitutional adjudications, I do submit that the formula suggested [by the dissenters] for achieving it is more hollow than real. ''Specific'' provisions of the Constitution, no less than ''due process'' lend themselves as readily to ''personal'' interpretations by judges whose constitutional outlook is simply to keep the Constitution in supposed ''tune with the times''. . . . Judicial self-restraint [will] be achieved in this area, as in other[s], only by continual insistence upon respect for the teachings of history, solid recognition of the basic values that underlie our society, and wise appreciation of the great roles that the doctrines of federalism and separation of powers have played in establishing and preserving American freedoms. Adherence to these principles will not, of course, obviate all constitutional differences of opinion among judges, nor should it. Their continued recognition will, however, go farther toward keeping most judges from roaming at large in the constitutional field than will the interpolation into the Constitution of an artificial and largely illusory restriction on the content of the Due Process Clause.

Justice William H. Rehnquist in his dissent in Doe v. Bolton (410 US 179, 1973) entered a caveat on the Fourteenth Amendment:

> If the Court means by the term "privacy" no more than that the claim of a person to be free from unwanted state regulation of consensual transactions may be a form of "liberty" . . . I agree [with] Mr. Justice Stewart in his concurring opinion that the "liberty," against deprivation of which without due process the Fourteenth Amendment protects, embraces more than the rights found in the Bill of Rights. But that liberty is not guaranteed absolutely against deprivation, but only against deprivation without due process of law.

The Sixth Amendment requires that "in all criminal prosecutions, the accused shall enjoy the right to a speedy and public trial . . . and to be informed of the nature and cause of the accusation . . . " It has been held that a "fair trial" implies recognition of the accused's right of privacy as well as the witness' right not to be harassed or embarrassed (U.S. v. Criden, 675 F2d 409, 3rd Cir, 1982). The privacy rights of witnesses and jurors have also been weighed in determining whether to open or close certain portions of criminal proceedings (Lexington Herald Leader Co. v. Tackett, 601 SW2d 905, Ky, 1980).

3.6 THE CONSTITUTIONAL RIGHT OF PRIVACY IN THE CRIMINAL SETTING

In recent years courts have commenced to recognize an amorphous "constitutional" right of privacy in the criminal setting, as illustrated by York v. Story (324 F2d 450, 9th Cir, 1963). Here the plaintiff, a female assault victim, was ordered by police to strip and allow photographs of her nude body to be taken; these photographs were then circulated throughout the police department. The court held that she had a tort claim for damages against the police department, arising out of their violation of her constitutional right of privacy. And in Price v. Shepard (239 NW2d 905, 1976) the Minnesota Supreme Court held that a medical director, assuming custody and care of a mentally ill minor pursuant to involuntary commitment, was subject to liability for violating the minor's constitutional right of privacy for utilizing electroshock therapy. The U.S. Supreme Court in Bivens v. Six Unknown Agents of the Federal Bureau of Narcotics (403 US 388, 1971) ruled that plaintiffs could recover money damages for violations of the Fourth Amendment by federal agents under color of their authority. The New York Court of Appeals in People v. Branigan, decided March 26, 1986, examined the parameters of the "reasonable right of privacy." Here two police officers stopped the automobile that the defendant was driving because the car "had a cracked windshield, void stickers, and no front license plate." Defendant stated that the car was not his and that he had no license to drive in New York; police ordered him and his passenger out of the car for "safety reasons." Inside the car was found two automatic pistols, and both persons were placed under arrest. Defendant pleaded guilty to criminal possession of a weapon, but on appeal contended that his privacy was illegally invaded. But the court affirmed the conviction: "In the limited circumstances presented by these facts, and in light of the diminished expectation of privacy with respect to the contents of automobiles . . . the officer was justified in looking for the document in the area specified by defendant rather than having to arrest him."

The landmark case of Monroe v. Pape (365 US 167, 1970) presents the instance of city police officers breaking into plaintiffs' home in the early morning, routing them from bed, making them stand nude in the living room, and ransacking every room including the emptying of drawers and ripping open of mattresses. Plaintiffs brought suit under 42 USC 1983, which reads:

> Every person, who under color of any statute, ordinance, regulation, custom, or usage, of any State or Territory, subjects, or causes to be subjected, any citizen of the United States or other person within the jurisdiction thereof to the deprivation of any rights, privileges, or immunities secured by the Constitution and laws, shall be liable to the party injured in an action at law, suit in equity, or other proper proceeding for redress.

Justice William O. Douglas, writing the majority opinion, found these invasions of the police officers to be in violation of the "constitutional" rights implicit in Section 1983, but that the city need not succumb to the federal legislation. The concurring opinion of Justice John Marshall Harlan stressed that Section 1983 was not limited to state-authorized unconstitutional acts. The dissent of Justice Felix Frankfurter was based upon the fear that Section 1983 would be extended far beyond its course:

> Of an enactment like the Civil Rights Act, dealing with the safeguarding and promotion of individual freedom it is especially relevant to be mindful that, since it is projected into the future, it is ambulatory in its scope, the statute properly absorbing the expanding reach of its purpose to the extent that the words with which that purpose is conveyed fairly bear such expansion. But this admissible expansion of meaning through the judicial process does not entirely unbind the courts and license their exercise of what is qualitatively a different thing, namely, the formulation of policy through legislation. In one of the last writings by that tough-minded libertarian, who was also no friend of narrow construction, Professor Zechariah Chafee, Jr., he admonished against putting the Civil Rights Act to dubious new uses even though, as a matter of policy, they might be desirable in the changed climate nearly a hundred years after its enactment: "At all events, we can be sure of one thing. If federal protection be desirable, we ought to get it by something better than a criminal statute of antiquated uncertainties and based on the out-moded Privileges and Immunities Clause of the Fourteenth Amendment. . . . It is very queer to try to protect human rights in the middle of the Twentieth Century by a left-over from the days of General Grant." Id., at page 529. It is not a work for courts to melt and recast this statute. "Under color" of law meant by authority of law in the nineteenth century. No judicial sympathy, however strong, for needs now felt can

> give the phrase—a phrase which occurs in a statute, not in a constitution—any different meaning in the twentieth. . . .
>
> This meaning, no doubt, poses difficulties for the case-by-case application of §1979. Manifestly the applicability of section in an action for damages cannot be made to turn upon the actual availability or unavailability of a state-law remedy for each individual plaintiff's situation. Prosecution to adverse judgment of a state-court damage claim cannot be made prerequisite to §1979 relief. In the first place, such a requirement would effectively mullify §1979 as a vehicle for recovering damages. In the second place, the conclusion that police activity which violated state law is not ''under color'' of state law does not turn upon the existence of a state tort remedy. Rather, it recognizes the freedom of the States to fashion their own laws of torts in their own way under no threat of federal intervention save where state law makes determinative of a plaintiff's rights the particular circumstance that defendants are acting by state authority. Section 1979 was not designed to cure and level all the possible imperfections of local common-law doctrines, but to provide for the case of the defendant who can claim that some particular dispensation of state authority immunizes him from the ordinary processes of the law.

Justice Felix Frankfurter's view came true, for the statutory provision has been used successfully in actions to reapportion legislatures, to desegregate schools, to secure welfare benefits, and to protest denials of local licenses, as well as to recover damages for the consequences of police action involving physical contacts and restraints. In Scheuer v. Rhodes (416 US 232, 1974) the survivors of the youths who died in the gunfire on the campus of Kent State University in May 1970 sued the governor of Ohio, the senior officers of the Ohio National Guard, and the president of Kent State University under Section 1983, and the U.S. Supreme Court refused to give defendants absolute immunity. The court defined

> in varying scope, a qualified immunity . . . available to officers of the executive branch of Government, the variation dependent upon the scope of discretion and responsibilities of the office and all the circumstances as they reasonably appeared at the time of the action on which liability is sought to be based. It is the existence of reasonable grounds for the belief formed at the time and in light of all the circumstances, coupled with good faith belief, that affords basis for qualified immunity of executive officers for acts performed in the course of official conduct.

But in 1976 in Paul v. Davis (424 US 693) the highest court restricted the possibilities for bringing suit based upon this ''constitutional right of privacy.'' Here the local police distributed to merchants a flyer characterizing the plaintiff as a shoplifter; after plaintiff was acquitted of shoplifting charges, he sued the police under 42 USC 1983, which allows recovery for the deprivation, under color of state law, of any constitutional right. Although plaintiff based his case on violation of due process under the Fourteenth Amendment, the court rejected his claim on the grounds that the Fourteenth Amendment protects only interests in "liberty" or in "property," and that one's interest in one's reputation or personality does not fall into either category. Stigmatization of an individual simply does not fall within the protection of the Fourteenth Amendment. The dissenting opinions contended that an individual's interest in his reputation, at least where what is at stake is an allegation of criminal conduct, is a "liberty" interest which if violated by government officials should give rise to a federal cause of action under Section 1983. In Fadjo v. Coon (633 F2d 1172, 5th Cir, 1981) the plaintiff alleged sufficient state action for a Section 1983 claim; plaintiff beneficiary sued the defendant and six insurance companies for conspiracy to violate his right of privacy. The Fifth U.S. Court of Appeals reversed the district court's dismissal for lack of subject matter jurisdiction, holding that the state, when investigating the disappearance of the insured, could compel testimony from the beneficiary of six life insurance policies, but the state's later disclosure of plaintiff's statements to the insurers could be sufficient state action to warrant invocation of Section 1983.

The sodomy penal statutes have been the subject of much litigation in constitutional challenges based upon the right of privacy. Section 130.38 of the New York Penal Law, for example, states: "A person is guilty of consensual sodomy when he engages in deviate sexual intercourse with another person," and under Section 130.00(2) "deviate sexual intercourse" is defined as "sexual conduct between persons not married to each other consisting of contact between the penis and the anus, the mouth and penis, or the mouth and vulva." In People v. Onofre (424 NYS2d 566, 1980) the defendant moved to dismiss the indictment on the ground that the New York sodomy statute was a violation of his constitutional right of privacy by denying him equal protection of the laws under the Fourteenth Amendment. The New York Court of Appeals agreed, as did the Seventh U.S. Court of Appeals in Cotner v. Henry (394 F2d 873, 1968; cert den 393 US 847, 1968), which held an Indiana statute unconstitutional for attempting to regulate the private, consensual behavior of married persons. But in Lovisi v. Slayton (539 F2d 349, 1976; cert den 429 US 977, 1976) the Fourth U.S. Court of Appeals ruled that the defendants' conviction for sodomy was proper because the right of privacy had been waived when defendants allowed a third party to participate in the sexual activities and permitted photographs of the activity to fall into the hands of their children. A federal district court in Maryland (Acanfora v. Board of Education, 359 F Supp 843, 1973) found the right to engage in homosexual activity to be a fundamental right of persons which is equivalent to the right of privacy. But in Doe v. Commonwealth's Attorney for Richmond (403 F Supp 1199, 1975; aff. 425 US 901, 1976) the federal district court in Virginia found no constitutional bar to the prosecution under the state sodomy statute of two homosexuals for their homosexual behavior committed in private. The court relied on the longevity of the state statute, the existence of similar sodomy statutes in other states, and the biblical injunction against such homosexual behavior. The dissenting opinion of Judge Merhige attempted to protect homosexuality by invoking the right of privacy:

> The right to privacy in sexual relationships is not limited to the marital relationship . . . intimate personal decisions or private matters of substantial importance to the well-being of the indivdiuals involved are protected by the Due Process Clause. The right to select consenting adult sexual partners must be considered within this category. The exercise of that right, whether heterosexual or homosexual, should not be proscribed by state regulation absent compelling justification.

In the criminal setting the right of privacy literally has opened the doors to the courtroom so that the press can report what occurs. In U.S. v. Brooklier (685 F2d 1162, 9th Cir, 1981) it was held that the First Amendment protected the right of access to pre-trial criminal matters; access to materials in the court records of criminal cases including discovery matter has been opened to press scrutiny (Brown & Williamson Tobacco Corp. v. FTC, 710 F2d 1165, 6th Cir 1983). The U.S. Supreme Court in Richmond Newspapers Inc. v. Virginia (448 US 555, 1980) opened the doors to criminal proceedings when it acknowledged the historic rationale for the policy of openness in criminal proceedings. In U.S. v. Brooklier (supra) it was held that the burden of proof necessary for closure of criminal proceeding requires the moving party to show that "public proceedings would result in irreparable damage to defendant's right to a fair trial, that no alternative to closure would adequately protect this right and that closure would effectively protect it."

On occasion the clergy-penitent conversation has been involved in criminal matters along with the right of privacy. For example, in State of Florida v. Mellish, the Florida trial court in 1984 held the defendent clergyman in contempt of court for refusing to testify in State court against a parishioner accused of child abuse. While the case was on appeal the Florida legislature in 1985 amended the statute so as to exempt clergymen from reporting child abuse cases. On the other hand, in California in Edwards v. St. Stephens Episcopal Church, the California Superior Court in San Francisco entertained a suit in August 1985 by a woman, who, after being convicted of embezzling $25,000 from her parish, filed a $5 million law suit against her priest, charging him with disclosing her confession to the police. It should be noted that the clergy-penitent privilege is one of the oldest and most widely accepted privileges.

3.7 RIGHT OF PRIVACY UNDER STATE CONSTITUTIONS

The constitutions of the states vary in content as to the right of privacy, some embracing First Amendment language, others embracing Fourth and Fourteenth Amendment language, principally. In California, under Article I, Section 1, the constitution states that "all people are by nature free and independent, and have certain inalienable rights, among which are those of enjoying and defending life and liberty; acquiring, possessing, and protecting property; and pursuing and obtaining safety, happiness and *privacy*'' (emphasis added). Florida adopted, in Article I, Section 12 of the Florida Constitution, the language of the Fourth Amendment, as did the state of Hawaii (Article I, Section 5) and the state of Illinois (Article I, Section 6). The Louisiana Constitution (Article I, Section 5) spells out the right of privacy in these terms:

> Every person shall be secure in his person, property, communications, houses, papers, and effects against unreasonable searches, seizures, or invasions of privacy. No warrant shall issue without probable cause supported by oath or affirmation, and particularly describing the place to be searched, the persons or things to be seized, and the lawful purpose or reason for the search. Any person adversely affected by a search or seizure conducted in violation of this Section shall have standing to raise its illegality in the appropriate court.

The Montana Constitution (Article II, Section 10) delineates the right of ''individual privacy'' as ''essential to the well-being of a free society'' which shall ''not be infringed without the showing of a compelling State interest.'' The New York Constitution, the first paragraph of which is identical to the Fourth Amendment, spells out the right of privacy in Section 12, Article I:

> The right of the people to be secure against unreasonable interception of telephone and telegraph communications shall not be violated, and exparte orders or warrants shall issue only upon oath or affirmation that there is reasonable ground to believe that evidence of crime may be thus obtained, and identifying the particular means of communication, and particularly describing the person or persons whose communications are to be intercepted and the purpose thereof.

The state of Arizona in Article II, Section 8 of the Arizona Constitution is very brief in its recognition of the right of privacy: ''No person shall be disturbed in his private affairs, or his home invaded, without authority of law.'' The state of Illinois delineates ''the right to remedy and justice'' in these terms: ''Every person shall find a certain remedy in the laws of all injuries and wrongs which he received in his person, privacy, property or reputation. He shall obtain justice by law, freely, completely, and promptly.''

Unfortunately, there appears to have been little judicial interpretation of these constitutional rights, except for the state of Illinois, which in Illinois State Employees Assn. v. Walker (315 NE2d 9, 1974) expressly qualified the right of privacy. In Forsberg v. Housing Authority (455 So2d 373, Fla, 1984) the Florida constitutional provision was held to preclude public housing tenants from enjoying a housing authority with respect to disclosure of information to new tenants. And in California in White v. Davis (533 P2d 222, Cal, 1975) the court focused upon the right to be free from governmental surveillance and intrusion rather than on the right not to have private information made public.

3.8 CORPORATE RIGHT TO PRIVACY

A fat, bald-headed old hustler and lawbreaker named Bernie Cornfield is about to make another fortune by playing on the gullibility of the American public. It may have been P. T. Barnum who said, "There's a sucker born every minute." But today it is Bernie Cornfield who is trying to prove Barnum correct.

The above item appeared in the *New York Post* in a column headed "Bernie Cornfield turns to the health business." The plaintiff alleged that not only was the item libelous but it also constituted an invasion of his privacy. The New York Supreme Court, New York County, in Cornfield v. News Group Publication, Inc., decided December 11, 1985, found that "a corporation cannot maintain a defamatory action based upon words published solely of and concerning officers, employees or others connected with the corporation unless special damages are alleged"; the court also opined that the New York Civil Rights Law "clearly excludes a corporate party from [these] . . . statutory rights." Furthermore:

As for Cornfield's invasion of privacy claim, the legislature did not define trade or advertising, but the courts consistently have held that an unauthorized use of a person's name is immune from legal redress under §51 if used to disseminate information of public interest, regardless of whether the publication is published for profit. . . . The courts have liberally and broadly defined public interest and newsworthiness and published print matter using a person's name need not be confined to only social and political affairs but also may include gossip and colorful escapades of well-known people (Papan v. NY Herald Tribune, 301 NYS2d 120 [1st Dept.], affd 26 NY2d 941, 1970; Glieta v. NY News Inc., 62 NY 2d 340).

Clearly, the Brady column, in addressing itself to the past and future business ventures and activities of Cornfield, a newsworthy well-known financier and businessman, was used to disseminate the information of public interest. The court, therefore, finds that plaintiff Cornfield has not properly pleaded a money damage claim under §51 of the NY Civil Rights Law. His cause of action, in this regard, is dismissed.

Since the concept and scope of privacy seem inextricably intertwined with the individual or a natural person, it appears incongruous that a corporation or any similar entity should enjoy the benefit of a right of privacy. A corporation or entity, for example, does not experience feelings or humiliation or outrage nor entertain thoughts of social ostracism. But a corporation or entity may have identical interests with those of an indivdiual or natural person; the corporation or entity may be adversely affected by the individual's loss of privacy. A corporation or entity has been permitted to assert the constitutional rights of members in actions for nondisclosure against governmentally compelled disclosure. (California Bankers Assn. v. Schultz, 416 US 21, 1974). In Tavoulareas v. Washington Post (724 F2d 1010, DC Cir, 1984) the court extended an informational right of privacy to a corporation. Here plaintiff, president of Mobil

Oil, sued the defendant newspaper for libel, alleging the falsity of newspaper articles that his son had obtained business benefits from Mobil Oil through nepotism. The defendant served broad discovery requests upon the corporation; and, after the trial, Mobil Oil moved for a return of its confidential documents, the disclosure of which would allegedly cause competitive harm. The court ordered the material sealed on the ground that the corporation had a constitutional privacy interest in the nondisclosure of 3,800 deposition pages. In determining that the corporation had a right of privacy the court relied upon General Motors Leasing Corp. v. U.S. (429 US 338, 1977) and upon Civil Aeronautics Board v. United Airlines, Inc. (542 F2d 394, 7th Cir, 1976), both cases being to the effect that corporations possess legitimate expectations under the Fourth Amendment of confidentiality in internal commercial information. In both cases, the petitioner was denied access to the corporate records. Nevertheless, "corporations can claim no equality with individuals in the enjoyment of a right of privacy," according to the Tavoulareas court. The privacy interest protected by the Fourth Amendment is at most a reasonable expectation of privacy which is not to be violated by unreasonable governmental searches and seizures. Yet here in the Tavoulareas case there was no unreasonable search and seizure since the information was obtained through legitimate discovery procedures. Therefore, the decision means that there is indeed a corporate right to informational privacy which would be invaded if the information was disclosed to competitors or to the public.

4

Computer Age Technology and the Right of Privacy

The right of privacy has taken on new meaning in the computer age due to the highly sophisticated technology that has permeated society. And yet many of the problems of protecting the right of privacy have traditional roots that are nourished by the modern environment. In particular, a survey here encompasses the following: Arrest Records at §4.1; Bank Records at §4.2; Cable Television at §4.3; Computer Crime at §4.4; Computer Data Banks (Private) at §4.5; Computer Data Banks (Government) at §4.6; Credit Reporting at §4.7; Electronic Eavesdropping at §4.8; Employment Polygraphing at §4.9; Employment Records at §4.10; Medical Records at §4.11; School Records at §4.12; Social Security Numbers at §4.13; Surveillance Technology at §4.14; Tax Records at §4.15; and Wiretaps at §4.16.

In addition to the foregoing, the changing technology impinges upon areas of individual privacy with respect to laser beams and their utility for eavesdropping on conversations; closed-circuit, concealed television surveillance; micro-miniaturized radio transmitters; subliminal and subaudial projection of messages in the media; sophisticated drugs that unlock secrets without a person's awareness and almost immediately; brain-wave recordings that increase the prospects of learning a person's innermost thoughts and feelings; and even personality tests that delve into the recesses of the human mind.

In 1964 Vance Packard, in his book *The Naked Society*, remarked that "privacy is becoming harder and harder to attain, surveillance more and more pervasive," and that truly the "individual is at bay" (page 10). The past twenty-two years have only compounded that threat to the right of privacy. What is required is a discrete legal discipline, "informational law," which bridges the competing interests of tort law, criminal law, contract law, personal and intellectual property law, and certain constitutional concepts. Individual privacy and the "public's right to know" must be balanced under the protections of free speech and press along with security of governmental informational needs. The silicon chip and solid-state circuitry which permit miniaturization have made necessary such a new legal discipline. The micro-computer is but another device which enhances the power of informational demands and gives rise to "informational privacy" needs.

4.1 ARREST RECORDS

The right of privacy issue with respect to arrest records generally arises from poor police security methods which allow exposure of the contents to unauthorized persons. The general rule is that an individual or his representative may inspect his own criminal arrest record, as indicated in the California Health and Safety Code, Section 11361.5, and in California Penal Code, Section 851.8, for example. A court may in California order such records sealed if the person is acquitted or if it appears that the arrested person is factually innocent.

The states of Connecticut and Florida require the erasure of all court and police arrest records, including photographs and fingerprints, when the arrested person is acquitted or pardoned or the case is not prosecuted (Conn Gen Stat Ann, Section 54–90, and Fla Stat Section 901.33). New York, upon the termination of a criminal proceeding in favor of a person, requires that all records of arrest be sealed unless the district attorney shows cause for not doing so or if the arrested person applies subsequently for a gun license (N.Y. Crim Proc L Section 160.50).

On the other hand, the District of Columbia takes the position that arrest records in police files are open to public inspection at all reasonable times (DC Code, Section 4–134–5). The state of Nevada (Nev Rev Stat Section 179.24) opens up arrest records fifteen years after a person is released from custody for having committed a felony and ten years after a person is released from custody for having committed a gross misdemeanor; but a Nevada prisoner may petition the court to seal all records for cause; thirty days after acquittal or dismissal, the arrested person may petition for court to seal the arrest records.

In the federal court system the Law Enforcement Assistance Administration in the U.S. Department of Justice is required, under 42 ESC 3771, to promulgate privacy and security regulations covering federally funded criminal justice information systems.

4.2 BANK RECORDS

It is generally unlawful for the bank or the state to disclose publicly a list of depositors or debtors of the bank, as illustrated by Alabama Code, Section 17 of Title 5. California under its Government Code, Section 7460, requires that a bank customer be given notice before any official state investigation can inspect bank records of any individual. Iowa does not allow data processing centers to obtain information concerning the account of any person unless such information is essential to complete or prevent completion of a transaction then being engaged in through the use of that facility (Iowa Code Ann Section 527.10).

In Michigan a bank may not disclose any financial records unless the customer has authorized disclosure or unless bank records are subpoenaed (Mich Code Ann Section 225, Article 11).

The Internal Revenue Service under 26 USC 7609 must provide a taxpayer with fourteen days' notice when it issues an administrative summons to the bank to inspect the taxpayer's bank records; the taxpayer has a right to intervene in the proceeding.

4.3 CABLE TELEVISION

Under Public Law 98–549 the right of privacy is protected in cable television by a series of requirements such as the code of fair information practices to which all cable operators must abide; cable television subscribers are given the opportunity under the code to limit disclosure of their name and address for mail solicitation and similar purposes. In no case may a cable television company release viewing choices, retail transactions, or other personally identifiable information about subscribers without written or electronic consent of the cable television subscriber. A cable television subscriber is given the privilege of checking the information for accuracy at any reasonable time, and aggrieved persons are afforded the right to sue for damages. Furthermore, a governmental agency may obtain personally identifiable information *only* pursuant to a court order based upon clear and convincing evidence that the subject of the information is suspected of criminal conduct and that the information sought will be material evidence, provided that the cable television subscriber first has opportunity to contest the claim of the govenmental agency.

In the state of Connecticut under Conn Sess Laws 84–305 (1984) the cable television subscriber is given similar rights in protection of his or her privacy; it is illegal to release subscriber lists unless the subscriber has an opportunity to delete his or her name, or to disclose a subscriber's viewing habits without the subscriber's consent, or to install security scanning devices without the express written consent of the cable television subscriber.

4.4 COMPUTER CRIME

The enormity of federal and state legislation on computer crime demonstrates the intense concern in the computer world about protecting the right of privacy, inter alia. Under Public Law 98–473 it is a felony to trespass into a computer system and receive classified information with intent to injure the United States; it is a misdemeanor to trespass and obtain information from a financial institution covered by the Right to Financial Privacy Act (1978) at §1.6 herein, and it is a misdemeanor to trespass and obtain information from an organization covered by the Fair Credit Reporting Act (1970) at §1.6 herein. Furthermore, under federal law it is a felony to trespass into a computer system owned and operated by the federal government or a federal agency and to modify, use, or destroy such data.

In the several states special legislation has been enacted to encompass the many instances of trespass into computer systems, as illustrated by Hawaii Revised Statutes, Section 708, which delineates the accessing a computer system with intent to defraud or to obtain money or get information or introduce false information or wrongfully damage or enhance the credit rating of any person to be "computer fraud," which is a felony or misdemeanor, depending upon the amount of money or damages involved. Unauthorized computer use in Hawaii is a separate crime. In Maryland "no person shall intentionally, willfully and without authorization, access, attempt to access, or cause access to a computer, computer network, computer software, . . . " except for personal home computers and dedicated computers (Md Ann Code, Section 146, Article 27). South Dakota under S.D. Compiled Laws Ann, Section 43–43B–7, punishes "computer hacking," including the use or disclosure of passwords, without the consent of the owner of the computer, and also punishes wrongful access, altering; or disclosing computerized information. In Illinois it is illegal, without the consent of the computer owner, to alter a computer program, to access a system, or to obtain uses or benefits from the computer (Ill Rev Stat Ann, Section 6–9, Chapter 38). Kentucky holds that access for the sole purpose of obtaining information is a misdemeanor, and a person is guilty of "misuse of computer information" when he or she receives, conceals, or uses any proceeds from an act in violation or the law or aids and abets another person is doing so (Ky Rev Stat Section 434). It is a crime in Nevada to use a computer without authority, to get personal information on another person, or to enter false information about a person in order to alter a credit rating (Nev Rev Stat Section 205.473).

4.5 COMPUTER DATA BANKS (PRIVATE)

Data compilation in computer data banks occupies a major position in modern society, and countless companies are actively engaged for profit in searching and storing information. These private companies hire vast credit services to search out and make available sources of financial data about individuals. (Even a telephone book is a data compilation which lends itself to commercial exploitation in the use of "commercial lists," but such frenzic activity hardly merits individual protection of privacy.) However, the computer data banks, which have tremendous impact on retention and reporting of information, have the greatest opportunity for pervasive privacy invasion, because they generally hold extremely private details of one's personal history.

From salary to marital status, from financial net worth to personal references, too much private information is readily available in computer data banks to operators who can simply punch in the proper code and with little restraint obtain this personal information. But there are legal restraints upon the computer data reporting company's right to disseminate, as illustrated by Tureen v. Equifax, Inc. (571 F2d 411, 8th Cir, 1978). Here the court held that investigations by a health insurance company following a claim for disability benefits by the plaintiff were not in violation of plaintiff's right of privacy because plaintiff had specifically checked a box for a "special health investigation" when making his claim. Furthermore, the defendant company had a privilege to retain the information because of a legitimate business need for retention of such reports to minimize the risk of extending valuable benefits and credits to persons submitting fraudulent claims and fraudulent credit applications. Plaintiff argued that the later disclosure of this information to other persons was an invasion of his privacy, but the Eighth U.S. Court of Appeals found that such later disclosure was neither covered by the "intrusion" nor involved in a "publication" which would otherwise bring the conduct under the category of "public disclosure of private facts" (see §2.7 herein). In Shibley v. Time, Inc. (321 NE2d 791, 1974) the plaintiff brought a class action in behalf of subscribers to publications and in behalf of holders of credit cards, alleging that the practice of publishers and credit card companies of disclosing their names, addresses, and other personal information was an invasion of the right of privacy. The Ohio court found no such invasion of privacy despite the fact that the information was obviously disseminated. On appeal, the court held that an actionable invasion of privacy would require the unwarranted appropriation or exploitation of plaintiff's personality; and that because no endorsement of any products or services had occurred in the mere dissemination of names, addresses, and personal information, there had been no tortious appropriation under Ohio law (341 NE2d 339, 1975). On the other hand, in Fadjo v. Coon (633 F2d 1172, 5th Cir, 1981), which involved an investigation of a beneficiary of life insurance policies, the court found actionable a violation of a constitutional right of privacy because the information the plaintiff had given to a state investigator under a pledge of confidentiality had been released by the state to a private insurance investigator.

4.6 COMPUTER DATA BANKS (GOVERNMENT)

Every governmental entity, whether at the federal, state, or local level, is engaged in searching and storing information in computer data banks. The Internal Revenue Service, the Social Security Administration, and the military, in particular, have huge files of information on individuals, as do state, county, and municipal agencies which maintain automobile license applications or birth and death records, inter alia. The Privacy Act (1974) set the privacy policy for federal government agencies including the prime right of the individual to see his own files. Generally, outside disclosures are limited except for routine matters, and both national security and law enforcement records are exempt from the requirements of disclosure along with other exceptions under FOIA (see § 1.7 herein). Under PA [5 USC 552a] benefits may not be denied an individual for refusal to provide a Social Security number, unless there was pre-1975 authority to demand it (see §4.13 herein). In American Federation of Government Employees v. Federal Labor Relations Authority, the Second U.S. Court of Appeals on March 24, 1986 ruled that the Social Security Administration (SSA) had committed an unfair labor practice when it refused to release the addresses of 2,000 of its employees to the union that they had chosen to represent them. The SSA had contended that under PA it was barred from releasing information which "would constitute a clearly unwarranted invasion of personal privacy." But the court in rejecting defendant's argument held that defendant had viewed the privacy interests of its employees "with unquestioning reverence" but had treated the union's need for addresses as "without substance." The court observed that an average employee's privacy interest in his address is "not particularly compelling" since addresses are often a matter of public record. Furthermore the addresses "were crucial to the union's ability to frame proposals for collective bargaining." Similar victories were achieved by petitioners in Vymetalik v. FBI, decided by the District of Columbia Court of Appeals on March 18, 1986 and in Howard v. Marsh, decided by the 8th U.S. Court of Appeals on March 12, 1986; in the former case, the petitioner was deemed to be entitled to his request to see the amended records, and neither subsections (k)(2) or (k)(5) of the Privacy Act could be used to exempt records compiled in response to his application for government employment; and in the latter case, it was held that the army commander who ordered his staff to examine the personnel files of an employee who claimed sexual discrimination did not violate the Privacy Act since the army was entitled to defend itself against the sexual discrimination claim.

On the state level Utah has codified the principles of fair information practices found in the federal Privacy Act (1974), and an individual has the right to contest the accuracy or completeness of his own data in the state computer databank (Utah Code Ann, Section 63–50–1). In Arkansas (Ark Stat Ann, Section 16–804) the state's information practices act states that personal information used by government for a purpose other than the purpose for which the personal information was collected can "seriously endanger a person's right to privacy and confidentiality," and that a uniform statewide policy is necessary. In Arkansas there can be no personal information system or computer databank whose existence is secretive or operating surreptitiously, and there can be no collection of unneeded or irrelevant data. A citizen may inspect data on himself or herself and challenge and correct such data; and such personal data may not be disseminated for other purposes without the individual's consent.

California under Executive Order B–22–76 (1985) opens up state files to the individual who is the subject of the files and grants the right to correct erroneous entries to the individual affected. There is even a state mediation officer available to handle disputes about the accuracy of such personal information.

Connecticut under Conn Gen Stat Ann Section 4–190 holds that disclosure of personal data from state computer data banks without the consent of the person affected is prohibited unless the state agency has need for the information in order to perform its duties or unless such disclosure reduces the risk of imminent injury, or a statute or court order requires disclosure.

Kentucky mandates access to any and all records of public agencies except records of a personal nature, certain law enforcement records, and several other important records (Ky Stat Section 61.884). But any affected person must have access to any public record relating to him or in which his name is mentioned.

The state of Minnesota (Minn Stat Ann Section 15.162) codified the accepted principles of computer data bank privacy and defined precisely the identification of those confidential personal data records which are not available to the individual. The legislation covers the state university, state agencies, school boards, local commissions, and local authorities, but not townships; each state agency has a person responsible for its computer databank and must report yearly to a state officer on provisions for individual privacy, inter alia.

Ohio's Personal Information Control Board (Ohio Rev Code Section 1247.01) is responsible for rules and regulations concerning the nature and character of state personal information systems; generally information cannot be disclosed without the consent of the individual affected.

Virginia's Privacy Protection Act (1976) prohibits secret personal information systems and collections of unneeded, inappopriate, and inaccurate information (Va Code Section 2.1–377).

In New York, the Freedom of Information Law is predicated on the principle that the public has an inherent right to know, and in Winters v. Smith, decided on April 7, 1986 by the New York Supreme Court, New York County, the requested records about bribery were deemed not to be exempt as "inter-agency confidentiality, law enforcement confidentiality, and unwarranted invasion of personal privacy." But the court took upon itself the responsibility of *first* examining those records, pointing out that "the governmental agency has the burden of demonstrating that the requested material is exempt from discovery. . . . [The New York law] creates a presumption of accessibility which may be overcome only upon a convincing demonstration by the public agency that a statutory exemption applies. . . . The exemptions are permissive, not mandatory."

4.7 CREDIT REPORTING

The Fair Credit Reporting Act (FCRA) of 1970 at §1.6 herein, gives consumers the right to know the nature, sources, and substance (except for identification of the investigative sources) of personal credit information (except medical data) maintained by a credit reporting agency, whether public or private (15 USC 1601). The protection of the person's right of privacy is implicit in such legislation, but the state of New York in Section 373 (1) of the New York General Business Law puts a heavier onus on the credit reporting agency, which in New York must have written authorization from the person before the credit reporting agency can furnish a credit report to anyone other than the person about whom the credit report was made.

California expressly gives consumers the right to sue for invasion of privacy in credit reporting (Cal Civ Code Section 1785.1) and also regulates the dissemination of information to the grantors of credit in California. Under Section 1786 every investigative consumer reporting agency which gathers personal information for reports to employers or to insurance companies is regulated; such companies must give the individual the opportunity to inspect visually all files on him or her except medical files which require the physician's consent. California does not demand disclosure of the sources of the information, however.

Florida prohibits collection agencies from revealing that a debt exists if that debt is in dispute, unless all the pertinent facts of the dispute are incorporated in the credit report (Fla Stat Ann, Section 55.72 (3) and (6)). Unfair credit reporting is a crime in Kansas (Kan Stat Section 50–720).

4.8 ELECTRONIC EAVESDROPPING

Electronic eavesdropping is a crime, and in the commission of the crime the individual's privacy is obviously invaded. The U.S. Supreme Court in 1942 in Goldman v. U.S. (316 US 120) reviewed the conduct of federal agents who placed a "detectaphone" on the wall of an adjoining office in order to overhear conversations in a certain lawyer's office. The court, relying upon the 1928 Olmstead v. U.S. decision (277 US 438), decided that such evidence could be used in a criminal trial against the lawyer, and that the right of privacy of the attorney against electronic eavesdropping depended upon whether the eavesdropping was carried on with the aid of a physical trespass upon the property of the individual being investigated, which it was not. But the test of "physical trespass" was repudiated in 1967 in Katz v. U.S. (389 US 347) when the high court ruled that "bugging" through an electronic device attached to the outside of a telephone booth was an unreasonable search and seizure in violation of the Fourth Amendment. The presence or absence of "physical trespass" is no longer necessary, and electronic eavesdropping is barred unless specifically authorized by court order or warrant. Courts have realized that electronic eavesdropping can penetrate individual privacy without "physical trespass." But the Omnibus Crime Control and Safe Streets Act (1968) at §1.5 allows official electronic eavesdropping with a court order or warrant (Alderman v. U.S., 394 US 165, 1969).

4.9 EMPLOYMENT POLYGRAPHING

Polygraph examinations have become commonplace in employment situations, although in recent years state statutes have endeavored to regulate or bar the practice. In Georgia, for example, polygraph examinations are limited to fifteen questions and no fewer than seven questions; all questions must be provided the interviewee in advance, and the person so examined is entitled to a written copy of the polygraph results; no questions may be asked about religion, politics, race and racial opinions, labor organizing, or sexual activities. The polygraph examiner may be sued for violations of the act (Ga Code Ann Section 43–36–1). But Illinois, under Ill Stat Ann Section 2415.1, allows polygraph examiners to ask about religion, beliefs on racial matters, political views, labor organizing or union membership, sexual preferences, or sexual activities when the inquiry is "directly related to employment." In Wisconsin polygraphs are permitted in employment situations if the person consents in writing, if the person is given the questions in advance, and if the person is given an opportunity to retake the test (Wis Stat Ann Section 111.327). A person may not be fired in Wisconsin for refusing to take the polygraph test. Texas requires that the polygraph test be voluntary and that the subject be informed of the results (Tex Rev Civ Stat Article 3313 (29cc)).

On the other hand, many states have simply outlawed polygraphing in the employment situation. In New York, for example, no employer may require, request, suggest, or knowingly permit an applicant for employment to take a test with a psychological stress evaluator or a machine that purports to detect falsehoods; neither may an employer use such test results, nor may a person administer such a test to an employee (Section 733 of the New York Labor Law). In Maryland, under Md Ann Code Section 95, Article 100, both private and public employers must include the following language on all applications for employment:

> an employer may not require or demand any applicant for employment or prospective employment or any employee to submit to or take a polygraph, lie detector or similar test or examination as a condition of employment or continued employment. Any employer who violates this provision is guilty of a misdemeanor and subject to a fine not to exceed $100.

Michigan also bars a "lie detector" or similar test of an employee, and precludes the discharge of an employee for failure to submit to such a polygraph test (Mich Comp. Laws Ann Section 338.1726). And the state of Alaska, under Alas Stat Section 23.10.037, prohibits the suggesting or requiring a lie-detecting test in private and public employment except for a police applicant. The California Labor Code, Section 432.2, prohibits polygraphing in private employment; Connecticut similarly bars an employer or employment agency from using a polygraph or similar device (Conn Gen Stat Ann Section 31–51g). But Delaware (Del Code Section 704, Title 19), Hawaii (Haw Rev Stat Section 378.21), Massachusetts (Mass Gen Laws Ann Section 19B, Chapter 149), Montana (Mont Rev Codes Ann Section 39.2–304), Oregon (Ore Rev Stat Section 659.225), Rhode Island (R.I. Gen Laws Section 28–6.1–1), and West Virginia (W. Va. Code Section 21–5–5a) all prohibit polygraphing in both public and private employment. However, the 11th U.S. Court of Appeals in Hester v. City of Milledgeville, decided December 11, 1985, approved lie-detector tests for *public* employees by asserting that public employees can be forced to take such tests, although leaving unanswered the question whether the results of those tests can be used subsequently in disciplining public employees. The court reasoned that "commpelled testimony" may be used for disciplinary purposes because the constitutional privilege to be free of compelled testimony against oneself under the Fifth Amendment extends only to "any criminal case" and not to disciplinary actions by the governmental employer. The lower federal district court (598 F Supp 1456) had in March 1985 enjoined the use of lie detectors as an automatic due process violation on the grounds that these polygraphs had been wrong between 10 and 49 percent of the time. The lower court had also observed that the particular way the City of Milledgeville had administered the test was invalid because it impermissibly encouraged employees to waive their privilege against self-incrimination in later proceedings. See generally 5 *Law Alert* 119 (1986).

It is important to note that the American Psychological Association in February 1986 adopted a resolution stating that scientific evidence on the effectiveness of the polygraph or lie-detector tests "is still unsatisfactory" (*New York Times*, February 9, 1986, at page 26). One of their reservations about the tests was that people who administered the tests "often have limited training and expertise in psychology and in the interpretation of psycho-physiological measures." Furthermore, there was an "unacceptable number" of mistakes that were made in reading the test results; even a trained examiner cannot make the test accurate more than 90 percent of the time.

The *New York Times* in an editorial dated December 8, 1985, purposefully took occasion to remind its readers that

> [t]wo million Americans each year are required to take lie-detector tests as a condition of employment. At least 50,000 are then denied jobs or promotions even though the results are unreliable. Now, after years of desultory debate, Congress appears convinced that this injustice is intolerable. . . . Organized labor has complained for years that companies use lie detectors to ferret out employees they consider to be troublesome or inclined to join a union. A more telling criticism, however, has to do with the effectiveness of polygraphs. They do not detect lies. Rather, they detect physiological changes that indicate anxiety. The human operator decides whether or not the anxiety is evidence of falsehood. . . .
>
> Almost half the states prohibit or limit the use of polygraphs in most private employment decisions. Critics say some companies circumvent state laws by taking employees

across state lines for tests. Congress can end the subterfuge and the injustices by passing Federal legislation.

Almost simultaneously the federal government, under the terms of a security directive signed by the President on November 1, 1985, ordered a "selective number of individuals who have highest levels of access" to undergo polygraph tests in order for the federal government to deal with espionage and other disclosures of information (*New York Times*, December 12, 1985, at p. A1). Among other federal agencies utilizing the polygraph in the employment situation are the Central Intelligence Agency, the National Security Agency, and the Pentagon, although other federal agencies are involved in such testing of the 2.5 million federal employees and the 1.5 million private contractors doing business with the federal government.

It should be noted that a 1983 study by the Office of Technology Assessment, a bipartisan agency that serves Congress, concluded: "The available research does not establish the scientific validity of the polygraph test for personal security screening. . . . While there is some evidence for the validity of polygraph testing as an adjunct to criminal investigations, there is very little research or scientific evidence to establish polygraph-test validity in screening situations whether they be preemployment, preclearance, periodic or aperiodic, random or 'dragnet.' " On March 13, 1986 the U.S. House of Representatives by a vote of 236 to 173 approved legislation that would prohibit most *private* companies from giving polygraph or lie-detector tests to prospective or current employees (*New York Times*, March 13, 1986, at page D4). This bill, however, authorized such testing for workers in day-care centers, workers in the production and transmission of electricity, workers in the manufacturing of dangerous drugs, and workers serving as security guards.

4.10 EMPLOYMENT RECORDS

Employment records containing personal information also pose problems in protecting the right of privacy. Intrusion is somewhat restricted where the employer is required to permit the employee to inspect all records and personnel files concerning himself or herself at all reasonable times, as set forth in the California Labor Code, Section 1198.5, and the California Education Code, Section 24317.

The content of the employment file in Maryland cannot contain information on an employee's psychological or psychiatric condition which does not bear a direct, material, and timely relationship to the employee's capacity to perform the job (Md Ann Code, Section 95A, Article 100).

4.11 MEDICAL RECORDS

Medical records are deemed to be extremely personal and even intimate in the sense that courts lean over backwards to protect such records from intrusion or invasion that adversely affects privacy of the individual. In DeMay v. Roberts (9 NW 146), an 1881 decision of the Michigan court, a lay person accompanied the doctor into a room where Mrs. Roberts was in labor and about to give birth to a child. It was evident that the lay person entered the room under false pretenses, and the blame was placed upon defendant physician, who had failed to apprise the plaintiffs that the person was a lay person not medically trained. Any tacit assent by Mrs. Roberts and her husband was inoperative, according to the court. The 1881 court termed childbirth a "most sacred" act and upheld invasion of privacy of Mrs. Roberts. A century later the unauthorized viewing of her medical records would similarly be deemed an intrusion or invasion of the patient's privacy. In 1977 in Doe v. Roe (400 NYS2d 668) a New York court enjoined a psychiatrist from publishing a medical book containing a detailed case history and verbatim disclosures from therapy of the plaintiff, the patient of the psychiatrist. The court upheld the claim based on the implied contract of confidentiality in a professional relationship and upon statutory medical regulations. (Note that there was no common law right of privacy in New York.) The medical records of the inmates of a state correctional institution formed the background of a film in Commonwealth of Massachusetts v. Wiseman (249 NE2d 610, 1969; cert den 398 US 960, 1970); and the court concluded that the film was "an undeniable infringement of the privacy of the inmates filmed."

The New York Appellate Division, First Department, in Y v. Kuriansky, on November 18, 1985, voided subpoenas of patient records in a Medicaid probe because there was no "particularized need" for such medical records. Proof of the dates and times of treatment by the psychiatrists, which evidence was vital to establish allegations with respect to the provision of medical services during periods when the psychiatrists were out of the country, could be obtained by alternate means. The medical records sought, if disclosed, "would be damaging to patients if known to others" and also would be "painful" to the patients involved. Reconciling the competing considerations, the court remanded the matter for an "in camera" inspection of the subpoenaed materials to determine if there was "particularized need" for the portions of the record that would otherwise be protected.

The states have by legislation generally cemented the physician's privilege in not disclosing the contents of medical records: New Hampshire (N.H. Rev Stat Ann Section 329.26 and Section 330–A:19), Oregon (Ore Rev Stat Section 44.040), South Dakota (S.D. Compil Laws Ann Section 19–2–3), Idaho (Ida Code Section 9–203 (4)), Indiana (Ind Code Ann Section 2.1714 (4)), and Kansas (Kan Stat Section 60–427), for example. But Hawaii recognizes the physician's privilege only in civil cases (Haw Rev Stat Section 621–20), and Georgia limits the privilege to psychiatrists (Ga Code Ann Section 38–418 (5)), but holds that disclosure of medical records in court does not destroy the confidential nature of the records (Section 37–718). Nevada allows the patient to refuse to disclose or to forbid another person from disclosing a patient's medical information (Nev Rev Stat Section 49.215–245). Tennessee holds that the privilege against disclosure exists only for the psychiatrist, and hospital records are simply the property of the hospital available for disclosure (Tenn Code Ann Section 24–112 and Section 53–1322).

In New York, under the New York Mental Hygiene Law, a hearing held to determine the mental condition of a person requires that "representatives of the news media shall be admitted subject to guidelines preserving confidentiality and privacy of the inmate, defendant or patient." Furthermore, Rule 694.7 (c) of the Appellate Division, Second Department,

> [r]epresents clear recognition that under certain circumstances the news media may be "properly interested" in judicial proceedings under the Mental Hygiene Law. Clearly, if the "news media" could never be "properly interested" in Mental Hygiene Law hearings, their presence would have to be forbidden categorically. We have difficulty in discerning a great difference—particularly in principle—between news-media presence at a judicial hearing subject to guidelines intended to protect privacy and news-media viewing of a transcript redacted to protect privacy. Presence at a hearing reveals all the testimony while a redacted transcript does not. If, as appellants declared during oral argument, the information permitted to be disseminated by the news media after their viewing of such proceedings can be limited by guidelines, so can the information obtained upon a viewing of the sealed transcript. Indeed, in this case, Special Term applied guidelines in prohibiting the viewing of certain portions of the transcript to protect what remains of Ms. Ventura's privacy.

In this decision, In the Matter of New York News, Inc., dated November 20, 1985, the defendant had been charged with attempted murder and assault for pushing a woman in the path of an oncoming subway train. Newspaper investigation had uncovered the fact that a month prior the defendant had been released from a psychiatric hospital after a judicial hearing under the New York Mental Hygiene Law. The news media applied to court for release of the minutes of that proceeding, and the New York Appellate Division, Second Department, ruled:

> We do not believe that permitting the viewing of a redacted transcript in a case such as this—where both identity, hospitalization, and other facts about Ms. Ventura are already public and have been widely disseminated—will erode the statute. Under the unique circumstances of this case, where the release of a mental patient was soon followed by tragedy and a heated public controversy over the Mental Hygiene Law proceeding that led to the release, the integrity of the judicial process would be significantly impaired if the entire proceeding were shielded from public view.

4.12 SCHOOL RECORDS

Privacy issues also arise with respect to information in school and educational records, as illustrated in Porten v. University of San Francisco (64 Cal App3d 825, 1976), where a student alleged breach of privacy when the university disclosed his grades from another school, despite the university's assurance to him that the prior grades would be utilized only for evaluating his application for admission to the defendant school. But the California court held that there was no disclosure amounting to an invasion of his privacy, in that his prior grades were only communicated to the California Scholarship and Loan Commission and not to the general public. But the court intimated that under Article I, Section 1 of the California Constitution the student might have a cause of action for breach of a confidential relationship. The state of Ohio by legislation precludes the release of student records for profit-making activities and requires parental consent to disclose the contents of a school record to another school for educational purposes (Ohio Rev Code Section 3319–321).

Today California students (unlike the decision in the 1976 Porten case, supra) are entitled, as students in public institutions of higher education, to the constitutional right of privacy (Cal Penal Code Section 626.11, and Cal Educ Code Section 49060). Parents in California have an absolute right, however, in both public and private schools, to see their children's school records. Connecticut gives parents the same access, but grants privileged communications status to communications between student and counselor, which even the parent cannot breach (Conn Gen Stat Ann Section 10–15b and Section 10–15a). Colorado, on the other hand, has opened up school records to employers and law enforcement officials even without parental consent (Col Rev Stat Section 24–72–204).

Iowa, under Iowa Code Ann Section 68A.7, authorizes the county superintendant of schools to release even the confidential records of present and former students. Texas permits the release of school records upon request of educational personnel, student, parent, or spouse (Tex Rev Civ Stat Ann Section 3 (a) (14), Article 6252–17a). Outsiders in Tennessee are authorized access to pupil records for research (Tenn Code Ann Section 15–305 (2)).

Oklahoma puts the onus of not revealing the contents of a school record upon the teacher, who may disclose the record if required for the performance of the teacher's contractual duties or when requested by the parent of the student (Okla Stat Ann Section 6–115, Title 70). It is a misdemeanor if the Oklahoma teacher acts negligently or intentionally as to disclosure of school records.

The state of Nebraska has separated academic records from school disciplinary records and authorizes the destruction of the latter records at graduation; but, under Neb Rev Stat Section 79–4.157, teachers, parents, and the pupil have full access to all the school records. New Jersey appears to favor liberal disclosure of school records with few limitations (NJ Rev Stat S Section 18A:36–19).

One interesting variation on the theme of school records and the right of privacy relates to the 1985 public uproar about testing for drugs among high school students in New Jersey. (See Odenheim v. Carlstadt-East Rutherford Regional School District at §3.4). Judge Peter Ciolino of the New Jersey Superior Court in Hackensack ruled that a school board policy requiring all students to be tested for drugs was unconstitutional on the grounds of invasion of privacy and unlawful search and seizure. The court held that the school board was trying "to control student discipline under the guise of a medical procedure. . . . The constitutional proscription against unreasonable search and seizure is not limited to only those who are suspected of criminal behavior. Instead, all searches by government officials, including inspections for administrative purposes, must satisfy constitutional-reasonableness standards." But, above all, the school policy "violated reasonable privacy expectations of school children" (*New York Times*, December 11, 1985, at p. B7).

4.13 SOCIAL SECURITY NUMBERS

The importance of Social Security numbers assigned to nearly every individual is highlighted by the widespread use of such numbers to identify individuals in every walk of life. The federal government has endeavored to restrict the overutilization of such numbers by requiring that federal, state, and local agencies must notify an individual of the legal authority that allows them to collect the Social Security number and to state what uses are made of the number (5 USC 552a (7)). But the Tax Reform Act (1976) has removed state welfare, tax, and motor vehicle agencies from this restriction. Nevertheless, under 26 USC 408, there are criminal penalties for disclosing or using a person's Social Security number contrary to federal law.

The Commonwealth of Virginia has made it unlawful to require a Social Security number for any activity or to refuse service if the number has not been furnished, unless disclosure of the number is required by federal or state law. (Va Code Section 2.1–385). But Virginia requires the number to appear on the driver's license of Virginia residents (Section 46.1–375); also, voters in Virginia must disclose their numbers in order to vote (Section 24.1–72.2).

4.14 SURVEILLANCE TECHNOLOGY

Surveillance technology today is extremely sophisticated, derived as it is from the hurried development of the transistor and the computer; the traditional electronic and visual surveillance devices have now been supplemented by tracking systems, to wit: the beeper transponder, attached to a moving object, transmits its signal to a central listening post, or the pen register records the telephone numbers dialed from a suspect's telephone, or the closed-circuit television camera surreptitiously peers onto the public street as police watch from a safe distance. Coupled with the dynamic changes in the methods of communication and in data collection is the convergence of communication modes, i.e., data, voice, video, and document and photograph facsimile copy, all of which can be channelled along the same microwave long-distance transmission belts via space satellite through fiber optic cables. Such advances in surveillance technology have also taken on the status of being middle-class electronic "toys" such as pocket recorders, portable television cameras, telescopic lenses to lightweight miniaturized cameras, citizens-band radios, the parabolic and directional microphones, all of which devices mean that more and more ordinary people as well as governments are engaged in surveillance, for fun or for profit. Super-secret federal agencies even have giant dish antennae that intercept communications traveling along microwaves across the world!

Computers also figure in surveillance, for a computer hooked up to a listening device can substantially improve the clarity of recorded conversation by inverting and eliminating the unwanted part of the signal, such as background noise and interference, and at the same time amplify the sounds. Computers can select individual conversations out of a crowd, out of a pack of telephone cables, or out of mass-data microwave transmissions. Computers can improve the visual image in video or photography; computers are used as giant storehouses and organizers of information and data that are readily retrievable. Apparently there is no federal law which purports to ban the interception of computer transmissions; the Omnibus Crime Control and Safe Streets Act (1968) proscribes the interception only of voice transmission, for example (18 USC 2510–2520). The privacy problem is self-evident, to wit: there is no law to bar surveillance or monitoring in public places unless the person subject to the surveillance is deemed to possess a "legitimate expectation of privacy," as delineated in Katz v. U.S. (389 US 347, 1967). Section 605 of the Federal Communications Act since 1934 bars interception and disclosure only of wire communications. But many states have recently entered the field by prohibiting "bugging" by electronic devices, such as New York's Penal Law, Section 738, and New York's Criminal Procedure Law, Article 700. Unfortunately, the landmark case of Katz v. U.S. (supra) was not concerned with the fact that modern surveillance methods are performed in public; that 1967 U.S. Supreme Court decision simply ruled that there was no privacy protection.

Electronic surveillance today may be illustrated by Smith v. Maryland (442 US 735, 1979), where, after the robbery victim gave the police a fair description of the robber and of the automobile, she began receiving obscene and threatening telephone calls from some person. The police spotted a man and an automobile meeting the description. Without a warrant the police had the telephone company install a "pen register" to record telephone numbers dialed by that person in his home, and the device proved that that person was indeed dialing the victim's number. That person sued the state of Maryland for invasion of his privacy by the installation of the pen register without a warrant. But the U.S. Supreme Court declared that plaintiff had no expectation of privacy in the dialed numbers; even the telephone company had facilities for making and did make records of telephone calls. Earlier in 1971 in U.S. v. White (401 US 745) federal agents without a warrant wired an informer with a radio transmitter and had him engage the suspect in conversation. The informer talked with White in his house, in a restaurant, in an automobile, and in White's house. Subsequently White was convicted of a narcotics violation, and the highest court found no violation of White's constitutional rights, despite the obvious aim of the Fourth Amendment to protect the citizen from a government system of uncontrolled and unjustified intrusions or invasions of privacy. In 1983 in U.S. v. Knotts (103 S.Ct 1081) police had reason to believe that the defendants were involved in illicit drug manufacturing, and so they arranged with the seller to place a "beeper" in the drug product so that the police could follow the defendants; subsequently the defendants were arrested and charged with the crime. Again the highest court held that a person has no reasonable expectation of privacy under the circumstances of the surveillance along a public way. "Beeper tracking" was thus approved as a surveillance technology replacing visual surveillance.

On the other hand, a warrant is available for investigative or law enforcement officers to undertake surveillance, and should be used. The federal statute (18 USC 2510 (7) and 2518 (1) (a)) permits such officials to make application for a warrant to a federal judge once the attorney general has approved the practice. A state like New York under Section 700.05 (5) of the New York Criminal Procedure Law permits application for a warrant by the district attorney or attorney general. The application for warrant must identify the applicant, identify the officer authorizing the application, and set forth a factual statement justifying the belief that the warrant should issue, because there is probable cause to believe that the individual is committing, has committed, or is about to commit one of the enumerated offenses. With a warrant in hand the surveillance by any technique can become lawful.

In summary, surveillance technology may be said to embrace (a) physical surveillance, (b) psychological surveillance, and (c) data surveillance. Physical surveillance involves observation through optical or acoustical devices of a person's whereabouts, his actions, his speech, or even his private writing, all without his knowledge or against his will. (See Samuel Dash, *The Eavesdroppers,* 1959.) Psychological surveillance embraces the use of drugs or hypnosis, singly or in combination, designed to induce revelation of a person's entire life history (including the intimacies) without knowledge or consent of the individual concerned (See 62 *Yale L J* 315, 1963.) Data surveillance incorporates the electronic data processing (see §4.5 and §4.6 herein) and other modern weapons for assaulting the informational privacy of individuals and groups of individuals with the result that under this onslaught of escalating data gathering and data disclosure the individual is steadily losing control over personal information. Professor Niblett in his book, *Computers and Privacy: Privacy and Human Rights* (1973), characterized the developing computer technology:

> These modern systems constitute a vast communication network for digital information in which the central storage devices can be interrogated and the data processed with imperceptible delays from many remote stations. By "on-line" is meant that communication is direct from the central processor to peripheral equipment such as teletype consoles and visual display screens. The systems operate in "real time"—that is to say,

the result of a processing operation is available instantly or on a time scale short by comparison with the process it is controlling or monitoring. The term "multi-access" indicates that the computer is available simultaneously to many users, who may be at terminals remote from the computer itself (page 1).

4.15 TAX RECORDS

The Tax Reform Act (1976) reversed the federal government's thinking that individual tax returns were public with certain exceptions: the 1976 legislation made individual tax returns confidential rather than public, again with certain exceptions. The individual tax return may therefore be disclosed with the consent of the taxpayer or his or her spouse; also, a written request from state tax authorities will be honored without notice to the taxpayer. Committees of Congress, the U.S. Departments of Justice and Treasury when engaged in tax investigations, and federal investigators with court orders, inter alia, may also have access to individual tax returns.

The states for the most part keep a lid on state tax returns by considering them confidential and privileged, as in Louisiana (La Rev Stat Ann Section 47:1508). No employee of the Department of Revenue in Kentucky may divulge information on tax returns or tax reports on any person except in a prosecution for filing false tax returns (Ky Rev Stat Ann Section 131.190).

The state of Wisconsin, while keeping tax records information generally under control, nevertheless sanctions disclosures "for publication by any newspaper of information lawfully derived from income tax or gift tax returns for purposes of argument and any public speaker . . . referring to such information in any address." Residents of Wisconsin may obtain for $1 the net income tax or gift tax reported by another individual or corporation, provided the taxpayer is informed of this payment within twenty-four hours. Even legislators, federal and local government officials, and any person with court authorization may examine tax returns in Wisconsin if done pursuant to the discharge of their official duties (Wis Stat Ann Section 71.11 (44)). In Maine legislative investigative committees and federal and state tax officials have access to individual state tax returns also (Me Rev Stat Section 5340, Title 36).

In Alaska the first case raising the right to privacy as a defense for failure to file an income tax return was State of Alaska v. Oliver (636 P2d 1156, 1981). The taxpayer argued that the right to privacy prevented the state from requiring him to submit his federal W-2 forms or other employer-generated records to the state for computation of his state income tax. In rejecting that argument the Alaskan court used a "compelling interest" test to the furnishing of information required by the tax statute, holding that the implementation of a tax system was a "compelling interest." The court opined that at best there was a tenuous connection between the information contained in the federal W-2 form and "a person's more intimate concerns," and furthermore the disclosed information was to be kept confidential by the Alaskan government (Alas Stat, Section

43.05.230). Thus, the privacy argument was lost to the revenue interests of the state. According to the note writer in 2 *Alaska Law Review* 159 (1985) at p. 177:

> Privacy is by definition a personal right, which involves the right to exclude an activity from society's view. Using society's expectations to define whether a given expectation of privacy is protected at all is fundamentally inconsistent with the personal nature of the right. The balance that must be struck in privacy cases is a balance between an individual's rights and society's rights. If society's expectations are used to define what the individual's rights are, the balance is bound to tilt in favor of society's interests.
>
> Society's expectations do have a role to play in deciding to what degree a given expectation of privacy will be protected under the sliding scale test. They should not be used, however, to decide whether a privacy interest should be recognized at all. If societal expectations are used in determining which interests will be protected, privacy interests will remain in a very precarious position.

4.16 WIRETAPS

In the modern electronic world wiretaps are considered passé, for wiretapping is more than a century old, although it was not until the year 1928 in Olmstead v. U.S. (277 US 438) that the legality of wiretapping was decided. The highest court then determined that the use of evidence obtained by wiretapping did not violate the defendant's constitutional rights. Done by law enforcement officers, wiretapping then did not contravene the Fourth Amendment against unlawful searches and seizures. But Congress had a different view and soon outlawed wiretapping by adopting Section 605 of the Federal Communications Act (1934), making wiretapping a crime if not done pursuant to court order or warrant. The right of privacy was thus legally protected by federal statute (see Lee v. Florida, 392 US 378, 1968):

> To safeguard the privacy of innocent persons, the interception of wire or oral communications where none of the parties to the communication has consented to the interception should be allowed only when authorized by a court of competent jurisdiction and should remain under the control and supervision of the authorizing court. (18 USC 2510)

At the state level, wiretapping is generally outlawed, as illustrated by the Alabama statute which provides that "any person who shall intercept, read, or in any manner interrupt or delay the sending of a message over any telegraph or telephone line shall be guilty of a misdemeanor" (Ala Code, Section 84 (18), Title 14). The element of "consent" was brought into Pennsylvania's statute, which forbids any wiretapping, even by law enforcement officers, without consent of both parties to the communication (Pa Cons Stat Ann, Section 5701, Title 18). However, the police may get a court order to wiretap for the protection of the police officer, but then the conversation may not be recorded.

Telephone companies appear not to be prohibited from wiretapping, but California requires telephone companies to keep a record of all devices for overhearing conversations that their employees discover, and the telephone companies must take ''adequate steps to insure privacy of communications over their systems'' (Cal Pub Util Code Section 7905).

Law enforcement officers in Connecticut have a big headache in obtaining consent to wiretapping; application must be made to a panel of three judges who must agree unanimously that there is probable cause and also that not more than thirty-four wiretap orders have previously been granted within the past year (Conn Gen Stat Ann Section 54–41a).

The tremendous number (estimated at 200,000) of cellular telephones in operation today has sparked concern as to whether wiretap statutes and wiretap decisions cover the new phenomenon. Cellular telephones employ radio rather than ''wire'' transmission and involve cordless telephones, which are especially vulnerable to privacy invasion. The popularity of cordless telephones in 1986 and the fact that a narrow range of frequencies are assigned to them make the problem of privacy even more acute. There is frequent interception, intentional as well as accidental, and it is probable that deliberate interception of cordless telephone communication is actionable. The eavesdropping issue is compounded when the interception is recorded or published subsequently, to the detriment of some person or persons. (See generally *New York Times*, March 11, 1986, at page B3).

5

Remedies for Invasion of Privacy

Courts may be able to grant several remedies for invasion of privacy, although in terms of pragmatism only the first remedy of damages (compensatory and/or punitive or exemplary) has achieved widespread recognition (see §5.1 and §5.2 herein). Other remedies include injunctive relief to prevent the harm (see §5.3 herein) and criminal penalties against the offender (see §5.4 herein). The New York Civil Rights Law encompasses all three remedies, while criminal penalties are delineated in Section 50 but limited to misdemeanors.

Section 5.5 herein raises the question of retraction of the invasion of privacy, when and if the retraction is physically possible.

5.1 DAMAGES: COMPENSATORY

The basic and pragmatic remedy for privacy invasion is the payment of damages as granted by a court with or without a jury. Damages are compensatory, but the measure of such damages is hampered by the "free speech" doctrine, which impedes the grant of large sums of money in many privacy cases, and by the fact that once the invasion of privacy has occurred and the embarrassing truth is disclosed (except for the appropriation of name and likeness which benefits the defendant), the judgment or award cannot undo the harm to the plaintiff that was caused by the invasion of privacy. However, in a few instances, large damage judgments or awards have had a chilling effect on defendants, whether they are publishers, movie producers, distributors of the media, or ordinary people leading ordinary lives. Still, courts are wary about putting clamps upon freedom of speech and freedom of the press, as enunciated in the First Amendment. The Hill family's right of privacy action based upon the publication of the novel *The Desperate Hours* is an example of what the "free speech" issue in the privacy area can do. The original jury verdict in Hill v. Erskine (240 NYS2d 286, 1963) brought the hapless suburban couple a total award of $175,000, of which the husband was awarded $50,000 compensatory damages and $25,000 exemplary damages, while the wife received $75,000 compensatory damages and $25,000 exemplary damages. Under the name Hill v. Hayes (18 AD2d 485, 1963) the New York Appellate Division, while upholding the liability of the defendants, nevertheless found the verdicts to be "grossly excessive" and reduced the husband's award to a mere $30,000 compensatory damages, but did not disturb the total award of $100,000 to the wife. The failure of the subsequent jury (and the Appellate Division) to grant the husband exemplary damages can only be based on the belief of the court and jury that there was no actual malice or ill-will on the part of the defendants toward the Hill family, but even that recognition does not explain the apparent discrepancy in awards between husband and wife. Four years later, in 1967, the U.S. Supreme Court reversed (Time Inc. v. Hill) on the constitutional grounds of free speech and freedom of the press (385 US 374).

In theory, compensatory damages compensate for embarrassment, humiliation, or mental distress suffered by the privacy invasion. Some courts are unwilling to accept the common law basis for the right of privacy, for the simple reason of not knowing how to determine the damages to be awarded. Ordinarily "reputation" injury should not be an element in calculating damages because injury to reputation is the key element in damages for defamation, and defamation gives rise to two categories of compensatory damages, i.e., special and general, which are defined in a way unqiue to the law of defamation and not involved in privacy actions. See Terwilliger v. Wands (17 NY 54, 1858), Erick Bowman Remedy Co. v. Jensen Salsbery Laboratories (17 F2d 255, 8th Cir, 1926), Curley v. Curtis Publishing Co. (48 F Supp 29, Mass, 1942), and Time, Inc. v. Firestone (424 US 448, 1976). In the state of New York compensatory damages for breach of privacy have been awarded for "laceration to one's feelings" (Grant v. Esquire, Inc., 367 F Supp 876, SDNY, 1973), for "mental distress and disturbance of peace of mind" (Manger v. Kree Institute of Electrolysis, Inc., 233 F2d 5, 2nd Cir, 1956), and for "property interest inherent and inextricably interwoven in the individual's personality" (Myers v. U.S. Camera Publishing Corp., 167 NYS2d 771, 1957). Compensatory damages will be presumed or inferred in New York from the mere fact of a prohibited use of a photograph (Metzger v. Dell Publishing Co., 136 NYS2d 888, 1955) even though plaintiff suffered no perceivable damage; the profit or gain or advantage accorded the defendant is the reason for imposing damages in favor of the plaintiff, in spite of the fact that defendant's profit or gain or advantage is an irrelevant consideration in arriving at a damage award (Cohn v. Loew's Inc., 135 NYS2d 550, 1954). The right of privacy action is indeed not one for unjust enrichment, and the defendant's knowledge of the invasion or intrusion is not a requisite element. See Welch v. Mr. Christmas, Inc. (440 NE2d 1317, 1982), in which the New York Court of Appeals relied entirely upon the language of the New York Civil Rights Law to find breach of privacy.

5.2 DAMAGES: PUNITIVE/EXEMPLARY

Punitive or exemplary damages are available in the privacy action when the representation or the conduct which invades the privacy was made knowingly falsely or recklessly. In Welsh v. Pritchard (241 P2d 816, 1947) the Montana court awarded punitive damages where a landowner, illegally occupying the tenant's premises, committed a series of "vicious acts," and the court felt inmpelled to discourage such outrageous conduct. (The plaintiff tenant never saw that money because it was merely offset against a personal injury claim of the landlord.) In Walcher v. Loew's, Inc. (129 F Supp 815, Mo, 1949) a former Army nurse saw herself identified in a motion picture, even though she was not identified by name; the Missouri jury found that she had suffered an invasion of her privacy to the tune of $65,000 compensatory damages and $225,000 punitive damages, even though the portrayal of the plaintiff in the film was hardly unflattering. The federal district court summarily reversed on the ground of the excessiveness of the jury awards.

The New York Civil Rights Law in Section 51 states that "the jury, in its discretion, may award exemplary damages," and New York Courts have readily approved punitive damages in the privacy action under the statute. See Fisher v. Murray M. Rosenberg, Inc. (23 NYS2d 677, 1940). But where the plaintiff waives the right to jury trial, the court may still award punitive or exemplary damages (Rosenberg v. Lee's Carpet & Furniture Warehouse Outlet, Inc., 363 NYS2d 231, 1974). The award of such damages under the New York statute expressly requires that the defendant had "knowingly used" the name and likeness of the plaintiff without the plaintiff's consent. But neither malice nor recklessness need be shown to uphold an award of exemplary damages in New York. (Welch v. Mr. Christmas Inc., supra). Evidence of the defendant's financial condition is very much relevant and material in computing the amount of exemplary damages in New York (Klauber v. SKE Operating Co., 295 NYS 701, 1935). Judge Samuel Hofstadter in his book *The Right of Privacy* (1970) summed it up in these terms:

> While theoretically the damages from the invasion of the right of privacy are the same whether the act is done by a rich man or a poor one, by a large and powerful corporation or by a comparatively small company, yet in practice, courts must not be blind as judges to what they know as men. It is obvious that the large and powerful corporation must be made to understand that the invasion of the right of privacy is an important element in the protection and promotion of the pursuit of happiness, and if the trier of the facts is unaware of the nature of the financial standing of the defendant, the damages imposed may not be substantial enough to accomplish the purpose of deterring the invasion. For this reason, general evidence with respect to the financial condition of the defenant

seems a logical ingredient of the cause of action for damages for the invasion of the right of privacy.

5.3 INJUNCTIVE RELIEF

Courts have been somewhat responsive to a plaintiff's request for injunctive relief to prevent the intrusion or invasion of privacy, but the "free speech" doctrine once again rears its prominent head to frustrate pre-publication censorship. In Cullen v. Grove Press, Inc. (276 F Supp 727, 1967) four correction officers at a Massachusetts institution sought injunctive relief against defendants who were about to exhibit a documentary film, *Titticut Follies*, about activities in the institution for the criminally insane. The film contained shocking sequences including a search of inmates stripped nude. The federal district court refused to grant temporary injunction against the exhibition of the film on the ground that the documentary film was not false or recklessly made in disregard of the truth. However, a Massachusetts court subsequently restrained general public exhibition of the film under the name of Commonwealth of Massachusetts v. Wiseman (249 NE2d 610, 1969). Similar restraints were ordered in Durgom v. CBS, Inc. (214 NYS2d 752, 1961) under the New York statute: "Regardless of what the equities of the situation may be and the damage to defendants from the granting of the injunction, a denial of injunctive relief for a conceded violation of the statute would emasculate the provisions for injunctive relief and cannot be justified." The New York court concluded that it would be unfair to limit the plaintiff to "the less satisfactory remedy of a damage suit."

Where there is no "free speech" issue, courts are more willing to grant injunctive relief, as illustrated by a 1933 case, Garden v. Parfumerie Regaud, Ltd. (151 Misc 692), where the actress Mary Garden was deemed by the New York court to be entitled to injunctive relief which would prevent the defendant from further marketing of a product bearing her name. See also Adrian v. Unterman (281 AD 81, 1952), where a designer successfully enjoined the continued use of his own name after the contract had expired.

On the other hand, in Albert v. New York Telephone Co. (204 NYS2d 36, 1960), where plaintiff's photograph was used without consent in the "Yellow Pages" of the defendant's publication, the only telephone directory covering Manhattan, the New York court denied injunctive relief on the basis that (1) it was impossible to recall the million or more directories and to delete the pages containing plaintiff's unauthorized photograph; and (2) the adverse effect upon telephone users and the business community of New York City would be staggering for more than eight months. The court balanced the equities and concluded that "to grant the application [for injunctive relief], the damage to the defendants would be by far greater than the damage to the plaintiff by denying it." The court thus frustrated the seemingly impossible demand of an overaggressive plaintiff seeking a quick, windfall settlement of his relatively minor damage claim. New York law nevertheless prompted a federal district court in Ali v. Playgirl, Inc. (447 F Supp 723, SDNY, 1978) to extend the scope of injunctive relief even to a foreign nation.

The U.S. Supreme Court in Spahn v. Julian Messner, Inc. (393 US 1046, 1968) raised the question whether injunctive relief afforded by the New York court in enjoining publication of an unathorized biography of a famous baseball player might constitute an unconstitutional restraint upon publication in violation of the First Amendment; the highest court did not need to answer, as the case was settled by the parties. In Commonwealth of Massachusetts v. Wiseman (398 US 960, 1969) the court denied certiorari on the same question, but Justice John Marshall Harlan (joined by Justices William O. Douglas and William J. Brennan) wrote a lengthy dissent:

> The balance between these two interests, that of the individual's privacy and the public's right to know about conditions in public institutions, is not one that is easily struck, particularly in a case like that before us where the importance of the issue is matched by the extent of the invasion of privacy. . . . A further consideration is the fact that these inmates are not only the wards of the Commonwealth of Massachusetts but are also the charges of society as a whole. It is important that conditions in public institutions should not be cloaked in secrecy, lest citizens may disclaim responsibility for the treatment that their representative government affords those in its care. At the same time it must be recognized that the individual's concern with privacy is the key to the dignity which is the promise of civilized society. I am at a loss to understand how questions of such importance can be deemed not "certworthy." To the extent that the Commonwealth suggests that certiorari be denied because petitioners failed to comply with reasonable contract conditions imposed by the Commonwealth, that question in itself is one of significant constitutional dimensions. . . .

Even upon rehearing the petition was denied (400 US 860, 1970), as was a similar petition in Doe v. Roe (420 US 307, 1974), when the highest court, having granted certiorari (417 US 907, 1974), dismissed the writ as having been "improvidently granted" in a case where a former patient was trying to enjoin her psychiatrist from publishing a book about her medical treatment. (The New York Appellate Division [345 NYS2d 560, 1973] had enjoined all distribution of the book until the litigation had concluded.)

5.4 CRIMINAL PENALTIES

Section 50 of the New York Civil Rights Law provides for a criminal sanction in the form of a misdemeanor, but generally there is "little realistic threat of prosecution" under the misdemeanor provision; see Time, Inc. v. Hill (supra). Very few cases have been brought in New York involving such criminal penalties, and in every instance the complaints have been dismissed (People ex rel Maggio v. Chas. Scribner's Sons, 130 NYS2d 514, 1954; and People ex rel Stern v. Robert R. McBride & Co., 288 NYS 501, 1936). The element of positive willfulness or wantonness required in criminal proceedings is generally lacking in privacy invasion situations, except where there is outrageous surveillance or deliberate exploitation of personality. In the McBride case (supra) the publisher of a book, *I Break Strikes*, utilized the photograph of William Stern, a person with a criminal record and apparently a strike breaker; Stern was not a well-known personality, and the court dismissed the complaint because it found no criminal conduct on the part of the defendant publisher. Similarly, in the Maggio case (supra) the criminal complaint charged the publisher of *From Here to Eternity* with invading privacy rights by the use of a name in the novel and in the film without Maggio's consent. In dismissing the complaint the court found that in no sense was Maggio the character in the book and film.

A state statute that criminalized the possession of marijuana in the home for personal use was struck down by the Alaska Supreme Court in Ravin v. State of Alaska (537 P2d 494, 1975). The court held that, given the fundamental nature of the right of privacy in the home and the limited potential for societal harm posed by using small amounts of marijuana in the home, the state failed to demonstrate a sufficient justification for criminalizing the mere possession of the product. There was no threat to public health or welfare which would justify criminal penalties.

A court may invoke sanctions against either party to an invasion of privacy suit if the court is of the opinion that one of the parties has not shown good faith in proceeding with or defending the case. In Leventhal v. Donahue, the New York Supreme Court, New York County, on March 16, 1986, was faced with a law suit by twin brothers who claimed invasion of privacy by the publication of a book "The Human Animal" following their voluntary appearance on a nationally televised show almost six years previous. While the court ruled that the twin brothers were "public figures" and that the book was concerned with newsworthy matters of public interest that are informative and educational, the court was disturbed by plaintiffs' reliance in their pleadings upon "misplaced" case law and rulings that were "reversed." The court wanted to invoke sanctions against the plaintiffs and their attorneys because the law suit charged "mischaracterization of facts, such as alleging that the challenged book 'portrays both said plaintiffs as having or suffering from some form of mental disease or disorder' when the book says no such thing." The court also criticized plaintiffs and their attorneys "for engaging in diversionary arguments" by raising a case dealing with physician–patient relationship communications, a reference the court termed "absurd." Nevertheless, even though the defendants here were "put in the position of addressing each and every claim of plaintiffs, no matter how absurd or lacking in merit," the court denied the motion for sanctions because of general restrictions upon penalizing parties for bringing suits "absent actual dilatory, successive or fraudulent practices."

5.5 RETRACTION

Under the traditional common law rule a demand by the plaintiff that the defendant retract the defamatory statement or retract the invasion of privacy, if it was physically possible, was not a requisite to recovery. But if the defendant retracted in some manner, this fact would be taken into account in calculating the damages, particularly punitive or exemplary damages. Some states, like California, have enacted "retraction" statutes that are tailor-made for the news media (Cal Civ Code Section 48a), and such statutes limit the plaintiff to actual compensatory damages unless the plaintiff demanded a retraction which had not been done. The state of Wisconsin (Wis Stat Ann Section 895.05) makes a demand for retraction a prerequisite for plaintiff in bringing his action. But a Montana statute which requires a demand for retraction as a condition of bringing suit was declared to be unconstitutional in Madison v. Yunker (589 P2d 126, Mont, 1978).

6

International Aspects of the Right of Privacy

6.1 INTERNATIONAL RECOGNITION OF PRIVACY

The British political scientist John Locke in his *Two Treatises of Government* remarked that ''Men being . . . by Nature, all free, equal and independent, no one can be put out of this Estate. . . . Every Man is born with a . . . Right of Freedom to his Person, which no other Man has a Power over, but the free Disposal of it lies in himself.'' The Lockian concept of ''right of privacy'' in a laissez-faire society does not ring true in the modern age of the computer, for today the right of privacy depends for the most part on the individual's ability to control the circulation of information as well as the conduct of others about him, a power which is essential today to maintain any dignified social relationship and individual personal freedom. Professor Lasswell in his *Conflict of Loyalties* argued that internationally there is a ''presumption in favor of privacy,'' and that it naturally follows from ''our respect for freedom of choice, for autonomy, for self-direction on the part of everyone.'' Lasswell summed it up in these terms:

> [P]rivacy is not just one possible means among others to insure some other value, but . . . it is necessarily related to ends and relations of the most fundamental sort: respect, love, friendship and trust. Privacy is not merely a good technique for furthering these fundamental relations; rather without privacy they are simply inconceivable.

In 1973 the Secretary-General of the United Nations in a report entitled ''Respect for the Privacy of Individuals'' reminded his world audience:

> Wholesale invasions of privacy inhibit liberty, often purposely. This is particularly true of surreptitious invasions, like electronic eavesdropping, spies, informers, entrappers, and psychological testing, the existence of which the subject is often unaware until too late. The community becomes fear-ridden, and no one can be trusted whether he be family, friend or associate; indeed, a person may be led to continual distrust of himself, as his efforts at individual self-fulfillment conflict with the norms of authority. This destruction of trust is one of the major dangers to a free society . . . the detailed questionnaire for employment, housing, insurance, and other matters, the hidden but suspected cameras in the washroom, the psychological tests, the lie detector and truth serum—all of these devices for ferreting out intimate and often unconscious details of our lives, produce a pervasive insecurity which suppresses individuality, discourages responsibility and encourages frightened conformity.

In the same report (UN Doc E/CN. 4/1116) the Secretary-General made the observation that "the very existence of an internationally-recognized right to privacy presupposes agreement that there are certain areas of the individual's life that are outside the concern of either governmental authorities or the general public, areas which may vary in size from country to country. . . . "

The Universal Declaration of the Rights of Man (UN Doc. A/180) states in Article 12 that "no one shall be subjected to arbitrary interference with his privacy, family, home or correspondence, nor to attacks upon his honor and reputation. Everyone has the right to the protection of the law against such interference or attacks." It is evident that Article 12 is a broad definition with a potentiality for further expansion, although Article 17 of the International Covenant on Civil and Political Rights does insert the words "or unlawful" to modify the word "interference" and thereby achieves a broader base (21 UN GAOR Supp No. 16, at p. 55). But both international agreements suffer from the fact that no definition of "privacy" is provided, and to the states or signatory countries is left the difficult task of definition, which always will involve conflicts with "national values" or "national interests" or with "national security" (8 *N.Y.U. J Int L & Pol* 387, 1975). Some semblance of "privacy" is found in Article 9 of the International Covenant on Civil and Political Rights, which provides that:

> 1. Everyone has the right to liberty and security of person. No one shall be subjected to arbitrary arrest or detention. No one shall be deprived of his liberty except on such grounds and in accordance with such procedure as are established by law.
> 2. Anyone who is arrested shall be informed, at the time of arrest, of the reasons for his arrest and shall be promptly informed of any charges against him.
> 3. Anyone arrested or detained on a criminal charge shall be brought promptly before a judge or other officer authorized by law to exercise judicial power and shall be entitled to trial within a reasonable time or to release. It shall not be the general rule that persons awaiting trial shall be detained in custody, but release may be subject to guarantees to appear for trial, at any other stage of the judicial proceedings, and, should occasion arise, for execution of the judgment.

4. Anyone who is deprived of his liberty by arrest or detention shall be entitled to take proceedings before a court, in order that that court may decide without delay on the lawfulness of his detention and order his release if the detention is not lawful.
5. Anyone who has been the victim of unlawful arrest or detention shall have an enforceable right to compensation.

Admittedly, the above five elements confuse ''liberty'' with ''privacy,'' although there are contained therein some of the long-cherished protections that extend to private life and the inviolability of the home. But ''privacy'' means more than freedom from unwarranted searches and seizures, as in the American Fourth Amendment; ''privacy'' delineates the integrity of family life, the secrecy of correspondence through different modalities, the protection against the unauthorized use of name and likeness, and protection against attacks upon honor or reputation. The General Assembly of the United Nations in December 1968 adopted a resolution urging the Secretary-General to undertake a study on the right of privacy and to prepare a report for the U.N. Commission on Human Rights to consider; of particular concern were the following:

(a) Respect for the privacy of individuals and the integrity and sovereignty of nations in the light of advances in recording and other techniques;

(b) Protection of the human personality and its physical and intellectual integrity, in the light of advances in biology, medicine and biochemistry;

(c) Uses of electronics which may affect the rights of the person and the limits which should be placed on such uses in a democratic society;

(d) More generally, the balance which should be established between scientific and technological progress and the intellectual, spiritual, cultural and moral advancement of humanity.

Subsequently the report prepared by the Secretary-General (UN Docs E/CN, 4/1028, Add 1-6 and Add 3/Corr 1, 1970) was considered by the U.N. Commission on Human Rights in 1971, and the Commission in its own resolution requested the Secretary-General to continue the study of the impacts of scientific and technological developments on human rights; and the U.N. Report on Privacy subsequently reported an inability to provide ''a concise international definition of privacy,'' although existing transnational prescriptions concerning privacy or private life are undergoing an expansion in general community expectations that will permit their application to many important emerging threats to civic order. The acute sensitivity aroused by the spread of sophisticated modes of surveillance, for example, comes at a time when people generally share an ever-deepening sense of powerlessness and of loss of individuality as they experience the power of multinational corporate organizations and the power of military takeovers in so many countries today. ''Privacy'' is becoming a potent symbol for a myriad of demands which functionally are demands for civic order and for the utmost practicable freedom of choice in the shaping and sharing of values.

The safeguarding of these human rights, including the right of privacy, is emphasized in Article 5 of the International Covenant on Civil and Political Rights (1966), entered into force March 23, 1976:

1. Nothing in the present Covenant may be interpreted as implying for any State, group or person any right to engage in any activity or perform any act aimed at the destruction of any of the rights and freedoms recognized herein or at their limitation to a greater extent than is provided for in the present Covenant.
2. There shall be no restriction upon or derogation from any of the fundmental human rights recognized or existing in any State Party to the present Covenant pursuant to law, conventions, regulations or custom on the pretext that the present Covenant does not recognize such rights or that it recognizes them to a lesser extent.

Similarly, the International Covenant on Economic, Social and Cultural Rights in Articles 4 and 5 stated:

The States Parties to the present Covenant recognize that, in the enjoyment of those rights provided by the State in conformity with the present Covenant, the state may subject such rights only to such limitations as are determined by law only in so far as this may be compatible with the nature of these rights and solely for the purpose of promoting the general welfare in a democratic society.

Nothing in the present Covenant may be interpreted as implying for any State, group or person any right to engage in any activity or to perform any act aimed at the destruction of any of the rights or freedoms recognized herein, or at their limitation to a greater extent than is provided for in the present Covenant.

Article 22 of the International Covenant on Civil and Political Rights also declared:

1. Everyone shall have the right to freedom of association with others, including the right to form and join trade unions for the protection of his interests.
2. No restrictions may be placed on the exercise of this right other than those which are prescribed by law and which are necessary in a democratic society in the interests of national security or public safety, public order (ordre public), the protection of public health or morals or the protection of the rights and freedoms of others. This article shall not prevent the imposition of lawful restrictions on members of the armed forces and of the police in their exercise of this right.
3. Nothing in this article shall authorize States Parties to the International Labor Organization Convention of 1948 concerning Freedom of Association and Protection of the Right to Organize to take legislative measures which would prejudice, or to apply the law in such a manner as to prejudice, the guarantees provided for in that Convention.

It should be observed that "derogation" from the rights conferred or recognized is always possible, as illustrated by Article 4 of the International Convenant on Civil and Political Rights, which reads:

> In time of war or other public emergency threatening the life of the nation any High Contracting Party may take measures derogating from its obligations under this Convention to the extent strictly required by the exigencies of the situation, provided that such measures are not inconsistent with its other obligations under international law.

Freedom of association, which is set forth in Article 20 of the Universal Declaration of the Rights of Man as "everyone has the right to freedom of peaceful assembly and association; no one may be compelled to belong to an association," and in Article 22 as "everyone shall have the right of freedom of association with others including the right to form and join trade unions, . . . " has an intimate connection with the right of privacy, as articulated by Justice Thurgood Marshall in his dissenting opinion in Village of Belle Terre v. Borass (416 US 1, 1984).

The World Peace Through Law Center, Washington, D.C., and its affiliated organizations of lawyers, judges, and jurists, at the Madrid Conference on the Law of the World, on September 20, 1979, adopted the following resolution:

> RESOLUTION NO. 11—COMPUTER TECHNOLOGY AND THE RIGHT TO PRIVACY. NOTING that the rapid advances in computer and telecommunications technology; NOTING the general usefulness of such technology and its advantages for mankind; and BELIEVING that such advances bring in their train certain risks to individual privacy and individual liberties that require the attention of lawmakers, RESOLVED
>
> 1. TO RE-AFFIRM the general rule that for the protection of privacy and individual liberties, an individual should be entitled in law to have access to personal information held about him, particularly in computerized data banks.
> 2. TO CALL for the enactment of national laws to provide, in accordance with local traditions and institutions, machinery to ensure ready and effective access by individuals to such personal information.
> 3. TO CALL for such laws, with such exceptions as are publicly stated, to make provisions on the following subjects at least:
>
>   (a) the statement of limitations that should be observed in the initial collection of personal information;
>   (b) ensuring the quality of personal information so that, for the purposes for which it may be used, it is accurate, complete and kept up to date;
>   (c) requiring that the purposes for which personal information may be used are made clear at the time of the initial collection and adhered to;
>   (d) laying down rules preventing the disclosure of personal information for purposes other than those specified, unless by consent or authority of law;
>   (e) ensuring reasonable security safeguards against loss, destruction, or illegal use of personal information;

(f) identifying a particular person who is accountable to ensure compliance with privacy requirements.

4. TO CALL for the development of international rules to harmonize national law and to facilitate enforcement of private laws on the one hand and mutual cooperation between countries to ensure the general free flow of personal information between nations, on the other.

6.2 EUROPEAN RECOGNITION OF PRIVACY

Since the year 1950 Article 8 of the European Convention for the Protection of Human Rights and Fundamental Freedoms (Europ T. S. No. 5, 213 UNTS 221) has guaranteed the right of privacy for "private and family life," for "home," and for "correspondence," but unfortunately the second clause of Article 8 places disturbing limitations or restrictions (or "derogation") upon that right of privacy, to wit:

> There shall be no interference by a public authority with the exercise of this right except such as is in accordance with the law and is necessary in a democratic society in the interests of national security, public safety or the economic well-being of the country, for the prevention of disorder or crime, for the protection of health or morals, or for the protection of the rights and freedoms of others. This Article shall not prevent the imposition of lawful restrictions on members of the armed forces and of the police in their exercise of this right.

Interference with the right of individual privacy by public authority can be devastating, as is so frequently done today under the guise of national security, public safety, economic well-being of the country, prevention of disorder or crime, protection of public health or morals, and protection of the rights and freedoms of other citizens. Even the bland prescription in Article 11, which reads, in part, "Everyone has the right to freedom of peaceful assembly and to freedom of association with others including the right to form and join trade unions for the protection of his interests" (213 UNTS 232), can be misdirected and rendered useless by the "exceptions" set forth in paragraph 2 thereto:

> No restrictions shall be placed on the exercise of these rights other than such as are prescribed by law and are necessary in a democratic society in the interests of national security or public safety, for the prevention of disorder or crime, for the protection of health or morals or for the protection of the rights and freedoms of others. This Article shall not prevent the imposition of lawful restrictions on the exercise of these rights by members of the armed forces, of the police or of the administration of the State.

The Declaration of Mass Communication Media and Human Rights, adopted in 1970 by the Consultative Assembly of the Council of Europe, affirmed that "the right to privacy consists essentially in the right to live one's own life with a minimum of interference. It concerns private, family and home life, physical and moral integrity, honor and reputation, avoidance of being placed in a false light, nonrevelation of irrelevant and embarrassing facts, unauthorized publication of private photographs, protection from disclosure of information given or received by the individual confidentially'' (Eur Consult Ass Res 428 at p. 911). Three years earlier, in 1967, the Nordic Conference on the Right to Privacy (31 *Bull Int Comm Jurists* 1) had concluded that the right to privacy or ''the right to be let alone to live one's own life with the minimum degree of interference,'' means:

> The right of the individual to lead his own life protected against: (a) interference with his private, family and home life; (b) interference with his physical or mental integrity or his moral or intellectual freedom; (c) attacks on his honour and reputation; (d) being placed in a false light; (e) the disclosure of irrelevant embarrassing facts relating to his private life; (f) the use of his name, identity or likeness; (g) spying, prying, watching and besetting; (h) interference with his correspondence; (i) misuse of his private communications, written or oral; (j) disclosure of information given or received by him in circumstances of professional confidence. . . .

According to F. Hondius, Emerging Data Protection in Europe (1975), it was not until 1970 that the Committee of Experts on Human Rights of the Council of Europe concluded that European laws generally failed to protect privacy adequately (pages 65–67), and therefore the Committee persuaded the Council of Europe to adopt in 1973 Resolution (73) 22 on ''the protection of the privacy of individuals vis-à-vis electronic data banks in the *private* sector.'' The preamble thereto reemphasized the fact that existing European laws for the protection of privacy did not provide sufficient protection for the individual citizen against technological intrusions of privacy. The Council of Ministers adopted the following ten principles as guidance:

1. The information stored should be accurate and should be kept up to date. In general, information relating to the intimate private life of persons or information which might lead to unfair discrimination should not be recorded or, if recorded, should not be disseminated.
2. The information should be appropriate and relevant with regard to the purpose for which it has been stored.
3. The information should not be obtained by fraudulent or unfair means.
4. Rules should be laid down to specify the periods beyond which certain categories of information should no longer be kept or used.
5. Without proper authorization, information should not be used for purposes other than those for which it has been stored, nor communicated to third parties.
6. As a general rule, the person concerned should have the right to know the information stored about him, the purpose for which it has been recorded, and particulars of each release of this information.

7. Every care should be taken to correct inaccurate information and to erase obsolete information or information obtained in an unlawful way.
8. Precautions should be taken against any abuse or misuse of information, and data banks should be protected from unauthorized access.
9. Access to the information stored should be confined to persons who have a valid reason to know it.
10. Statistical data should be released only in aggregate form and in such a way that it is impossible to link the information to a particular person.

See generally 18 *Gonzaga Law Review* 567 (1982/83) at pp. 593–594 and 17 *NYU J of Internat L and Pol* 893 (Summer 1985).

One year later Resolution (74) 29 of the Council of Europe urged member states to apply the recommendations of Resolution (73) 22 to the *public* sector. On January 28, 1981 the Council of Europe completed and opened for signature its "Convention for the Protection of Individuals with Regard to Automatic Processing of Personal Data" (Europ T.S. No. 108). The purpose of the convention was to protect the fundamental freedoms of every individual "with regard to automatic processing of personal data relating to him" (Article 1). The convention required signatory states to take appropriate measures including the enactment of new laws to safeguard personal data (Article 4 [1]), and to prevent the accidental or unauthorized destruction of personal data (Article 7). The convention covers both the private and public sectors. All personal data stored must be based upon legitimate reasons (Article 5 [a]), and must be accurate and in a form which permits personal identification only when such identification is relevant to the task for which the data is used. (Article 5 [e]). The convention forbids the processing of information on an individual's race, political or religious beliefs, health, sexual preference, or criminal record unless "domestic law provides appropriate safeguards" (Article 6). Once the convention has been duly brought into force, it will bind the 21 member states and will hopefully assure data protection in those countries where privacy is not adequately recognized despite the pronouncements by the Council of Europe. In general, some European privacy laws are more specific about government responsibility for record-keeping than Council of Europe declarations.

Sweden was the first European nation to enact a data protection law. In 1973 the Swedish Data Bank Statute (5 Computer L Serv [Callaghan] App 9–5.2a) called for the creation of a state administrative agency from which permission must be obtained before any person or organization in the private sector may establish or continue to manage a personal information system. The Swedish Data Inspection Board grants or withholds permission to establish and maintain personal files by automatic data processing equipment, and issues regulations as to the methodology so as to preclude the risk of undue encroachment upon personal privacy. These regulations supervise the notification process for advising persons whose data is kept, the personal data that may be made accessible, the methodology for collecting such data, the dissemination, preservation, and other uses of such personal data, as well as its control and security. Criminal records, political or religious views, information regarding psychiatric treatment or mental retardation, or any information pertaining to a person's illness or state of health can only be collected and maintained under specially approved circumstances. Inaccurate personal data must be corrected, and incomplete personal data must be completed. Every effort must be made to avoid disclosure which would result in undue encroachment upon personal privacy (See 18 *Gonzaga Law Review* 567, 1982–3, at pp. 594 et seq). The Swedish Data Bank Act also provides for a right of recovery in damages on behalf of the individual whose right of privacy is violated; and damages may include compensation for pecuniary losses, for mental suffering, and for other non-pecuniary elements of damages.

The Swedish Act served as a model for other European countries concerned with protecting the privacy of its citizens, and within four years West Germany, France, and Denmark followed suit.

West Germany, or the Federal Republic of Germany, had in 1970 a data protection law, the Data Protection Act of the Land of Hesse (1970 Gesetz-und Vorordnumnsblatt (GVBI) I.S. 625–627), but it was not a federal statute and applied only to the public sector. However, the West German Constitution of 1949 formally provided for the protection of "the free development of one's personality" as a fundamental right under Article 2, as follows:

1. Everyone shall have the right to the free development of his personality insofar as he does not violate the rights of others or offend against the constitutional order or the moral code.
2. Everyone shall have the right to life and to inviolability of his person. The freedom of the individual shall be inviolable. These rights may only be encroached upon pursuant to a law.

The West German definition of "privacy" thus embraces "a right to develop one's personality," which includes freedom to earn a living as well as to participate in cultural, religious, and educational activities; "a right to defend one's personality," which includes protection of one's body and mind as well as intellectual property; and "a right to defend one's individuality," which includes one's honor and reputation as well as one's intimacy in letters and diaries.

In 1976 the West Germany Federal Data Protection Law (BDSG) was enacted to insure against the misuse of personal data during storage, communication, modification, and erasure, and thereby to prevent harm to any personal interests that warrant attention (5 *Computer L Serv* [Callaghan] app 9–5.2a). The statute entitles every person to view all stored data about himself, to correct all such personal data, to block the storage of such data where the data are inaccurate or incomplete, and even to erase stored data under certain conditions:

> The storage of personal data is permissible if it serves the purpose of a contractual relationship or a quasi-contractual relationship of trust with the person concerned or insofar as it is necessary in order to safeguard the legitimate interests of the storage unit and provided there is no reason to suppose that interests of the person concerned warranting protection will be harmed. By way of derogation from the first sentence storage shall be permissible by non-automatic methods provided that the data are derived directly from generally accessible sources.
>
> The communication of personal data shall be permissible if it serves the purpose of a contractual relationship or quasi-contractual relationship of trust with the person concerned or insofar as it is necessary in order to safeguard the legitimate interests of the communicating unit or of a third person or of the general public and provided that interests of the person concerned warranting protection are not harmed thereby.
>
> The person concerned shall be informed when data concerning his person are stored for the first time, unless he has gained knowledge of such storage by other means. The person concerned may demand information on stored data relating to his person. Where the data are processed automatically, the person concerned may also request information on the persons and establishments to which his data are regularly communicated. He shall give details of the type of personal data on which information is to be provided. The information shall be provided in writing unless, by reason of special circumstances, some other form of communication is appropriate.

Unfortunately, the West German statute, also identified as the "Act on the Protection of Personal Data Against Misuse in Data Processing," which became effective in 1978, protects only personal data and not data relating to legal persons; it does not provide for any personal redress for invasion of privacy. (Schlesinger, *Comparative Law*, 4th ed., 1980, at page 579).

France delineates privacy in terms of "droits de la personnalite," which is perhaps broader than mere privacy, for it encompasses interests in the very notion of individuality, interests in bodily integrity, and interests relating to moral elements of the personality. (See Stromholm, *Right of Privacy and Rights of the Personality: A Comparative Survey*, 1967.) In 1978 France passed legislation entitled Law No. 78–17 of January 6, 1978, Concerning Data Processing, Files, and Liberty (5 *Computer L Serv* [Callaghan] app 9–5.2a), which requires that data processing be conducted in such a manner that it may not cause harm to human identity or to private life or to individual or public liberty. Some of the basic provisions of this comprehensive French law are (1) the collection of personal data by any fraudulent, unfair, or illicit means is forbidden (Article 25); (2) any individual has the right to contest any personal data being collected that are inaccurate or incomplete (Article 26); (3) the individual must be informed as to the identity of recipients of any personal data (Article 27); (4) personal data must be made secure against disclosure as well as against distortion, damage, or communication to wrong parties (Article 29); (5) the individual is entitled to view the personal data collected about him (Article 35); and (6) the burden of not violating personal privacy rests squarely upon the "data processing entity, unless it can be shown that such information was obtained directly from the person concerned.'' French law does not provide for a personal right of action for the injured person.

Norway legislated in 1977 its Privacy Act (5 *Computer L Serv* [Callaghan] app 9–5.2a), which expressly provides for fines that may be imposed upon persons or enterprises that in personal data processing violate the individual right of privacy.

Austria's view is set forth in its Privacy Act of 1978 (5 *Computer L Serv* [Callaghan] app 9–5.2a) and similarly provides for a personal right of action to the injured individual; the person whose privacy was invaded by the improper collection, storage, or disclosure of personal data may recover damages or even obtain injunctive relief.

England, strange as it may appear, does not recognize a right of privacy or a right to be left alone. But as an adjunct to the protection of other interests, English law does provide protection against unwarranted intrusion into private life as well as misuse of private information, as illustrated by the trespass cases of Hurst v. Picture Theatres, Ltd. (1 KB 1, 1915) and of Wilkinson v. Downton (2 QB 57, 1986); in the injurious falsehood case of Ratcliffe v. Evans (2 QB 524, 1892); in the nuisance case of Hubbard v. Pitt (3 All E. R. 1, 1975); in the conspiracy and economic torts case of D. P. P. Withers (A. C. 842, 1975); and in the action for breach of copyright of Williams v. Settle (2 All E. R. 806, 1960). In addition to these *implicit* remedies, there is equitable jurisdiction to restrain by injunction a breach of confidence, as illustrated by Attorney General v. Jonathan Cape, Ltd. (3 All E. R. 484, 1975). Here the Attorney General sought an injunction to restrain publication of the political diaries of Richard Crossman, a cabinet minister in the Labour government, 1964–1970. But Lord Widgery, C. J., refused the injunction on the ground that after a lapse of ten years, the public interest did not require the information to be kept confidential:

> However, the Attorney-General has a powerful reinforcement for his argument in the developing equitable doctrine that a man shall not profit from the wrongful publication of information received by him in confidence . . .
>
> It is evident that there cannot be a single rule governing the publication of such a variety of matters. In these actions we are concerned with the publication of diaries at a time when 11 years have expired since the first recorded events. The Attorney-General must show (a) that such publication would be a breach of confidence; (b) that the public interest requires that the publication be restrained; and (c) that there are no other facets of the public interest contradictory to and more compelling than that relied on. Moreover, the court, when asked to restrain such a publication, must closely examine the extent to which relief is necessary to ensure that restrictions are not imposed beyond the strict requirement of public need . . .
>
> There must, however, be a limit in time after which the confidential character of the information, and the duty of the court to restrain publication, will lapse. Since the conclusion of the hearing in this case I have had the opportunity to read the whole of volume 1 of the diaries, and my considered view is that I cannot believe that the pub-

lication at this interval of anything in volume 1 would inhibit free discussion in the cabinet of today, even though the individuals involved are the same, and the national problems have a distressing similarity with those of a decade ago. It is unnecessary to elaborate the evils which might flow if at the close of a cabinet meeting a minister proceeded to give the press an analysis of the voting, but we are dealing in this case with a disclosure of information nearly 10 years later. . . .

The trespass case of Hurst v. Picture Theatres, Ltd. (supra) involved a theatregoer who had been ejected by the management before the end of the film. Management argued that they were entitled to call on patrons to leave at any time and without giving reasons. But the court awarded damages for assault and false imprisonment. As Buckley, L. J., opined:

The defendants had, I think, for value contracted that the plaintiff should see a certain spectacle from its commencement to its termination. They broke that contract and it was a tort on their part to remove him. They committed an assault upon him in law. It was not of a violent kind, because, like a wise man, the plaintiff gave way to superior force and left the theatre. They sought to justify the assault by saying that they were entitled to remove him because he had not paid. He had paid, the jury have so found. Failing on that question of fact, they say that they were entitled to remove him because his license was revocable. In my opinion, it was not. There was, I think, no justification for the assault here committed. Under the circumstances it was for the jury to give him such a sum as was right for the assault which was committed upon him, and for the serious indignity to a gentleman of being seized and treated in this way in a place of public resort. The jury have found that he was originally in the theatre as a spectator, that the assault was committed upon him, and that it was a wrongful act.

And in the trespass to the person case of Wilkinson v. Downton (supra) the defendant, in a very jocular mood, told the plaintiff that her husband was injured in an accident, that both of his legs were broken, and that she should board a taxi to pick him off the street now. The utter falsity of these representations prompted the court to award damages:

The effect of the statement on the plaintiff was a violent shock to her nervous system, producing vomiting and other more serious and permanent physical consequences at one time threatening her reason, and entailing weeks of suffering and incapacity to her as well as expense to her husband for medical attendance. These consequences were not in any way the result of previous ill-health or weakness of constitution; nor was there any evidence of predisposition to nervous shock or any other idiosyncrasy. . . . The defendant has, as I assume for the moment, wilfully done an act calculated to cause physical harm to the plaintiff—that is to say, to infringe her legal right to personal safety, and has in fact thereby, caused physical harm to her. That proposition without more appears to me to state a good cause of action, there being no justification alleged for the act. This wilfull injuria is in law malicious, although no malicious purpose to cause the harm which was caused nor any motive of spite is imputed to the defendant. . . .

In the injurious falsehood case of Ratcliffe v. Evans (supra) the defendant had published in the local newspaper that plaintiff's firm had gone out of business, which was untrue; the jury found that the words, although not defamatory, were published in "mala fide," and awarded small damages.

The English practice of recognizing the right of privacy only in the context of another tort is further shown by the concept of "parasitic damages," which was defined by Lord Denning in Spartan Steel & Alloys, Ltd. v. Martin (1 QB 27, 1973) in these terms:

> [T]here are some heads of damage which, if they stood alone, would not be recoverable; but, nevertheless, if they could be annexed to some other legitimate claim for damages, might yet be recoverable. They are said to be "parasitic" because, like a parasite, in biology, they cannot exist on their own, but depend on others for their life and nourishment. . . . I do not like this doctrine of "parasitic damages." I do not like the very word "parasite." A "parasite" is one who is a useless hanger-on sucking the substance out of others. "Parasitic" is the adjective derived from it. It is a term of abuse. It is an opprobrious epithet. The phrase "parasitic damages" conveys to my mind the idea of damages which ought not in justice to be awarded, but which somehow or other have been allowed to get through by hanging onto others. If such be the concept underlying the doctrine, then the sooner it is got rid of the better. It has never been used in any case up until now. It has only appeared hitherto in the textbooks. I hope it will disappear from them after this case.

After fifteen years of national debate England adopted in 1984 the Data Protection Act (Chapter 35 of 1984), which allows an individual to exercise some control over personal information stored in computer files. Specifically, Section 21 of the Act requires data users to inform the individuals concerned when data is stored and to provide such individuals with copies of the stored information. The Act establishes a regulatory scheme governing transfers of information outside of England, and directs a data registrar to maintain records on all data users including names and addresses of persons in the countries and places outside England to which the users send information (Section 4[3]). The data registrar may enjoin data transfers in the interest of protecting the privacy of natural persons after the data registrar has determined that such restriction is in keeping with the "general desirability of facilitating the free transfer of data between the United Kingdom and other states and territories." (Section 12[4]). The data must be accurate and properly filed, and the Act allows an individual to recover damages if he or she suffers a loss as a result of the storage of inaccurate data on him or herself (Section 22). But the Act under Section 39 does not cover data users outside the United Kingdom, and therefore data processing conducted by multinational corporations, for example, is not covered if it is completed outside of England (Section 39[5]).

Belgium enacted a Privacy Act in 1977 that protects an individual's right of privacy by precluding disclosure of information about a person's philosophical, political, or religious beliefs; insurance coverage; union affiliation, cultural interests; and criminal record (Articles 24 and 25). The Act prescribes notification procedures under which the data bank owner must inform all persons about whom data are stored of the conditions under which access to the data bank will be granted (Article 26).

Luxembourg has a data protection law extending the right of privacy to corporations (*Journal Officiel du Grand-Duche de Luxembourg*, 11 Apr 1979). The statute protects against the abusive use of data collected for computer processing purposes when the data are communicated to a third party (Article 2). The law extends to foreigners seeking information from any Luxembourg data bank even if the data are used abroad. (Article 5[2]). As a result, if a foreign corporation seeks information about a delinquent Luxembourg customer, authorization must come from the appropriate Minister in the government. The law protects legal persons as well as natural persons on the premise that human rights protection extends to all, although the policy of preserving the confidentiality of business data is another important reason.

6.3 ISRAELI RECOGNITION OF PRIVACY

The modern state of Israel, according to one Israeli writer, follows the American development in the law of privacy (Carol Farhi, "Data Banks and the Individual: Is the Problem Privacy?," 5 *Israel L Rev* 542, 1970) because under "the traditional English approach . . . no such right exists." Another Israeli scholar, however, has pointed out that it

> is apparent that a number of basic elements of privacy are as ancient as Jewish law itself. The roots are already found in the Bible. Clearly in the course of time the right received classification and crystallized into manifest vested legal rights with civil and criminal sanctions.

(Rackover, *The Protection of Privacy in Jewish Law*, 1970). Dr. Simon Rackover concluded:

> It is quite clear that the employment of technological devices that make possible audible and recording surveillance, even though such devices are not attached to the property of the person concerned, falls within the complex of acts prejudicial of privacy which are prohibited under Jewish law.

Dr. Shmuel Shilo, head of the Institute for Research in Jewish Law, Faculty of Law at the Hebrew University in Jerusalem, has delineated right of privacy as subject to the Jewish legal principle of "kofin al midat S'dom," i.e., if "A" has a certain legal right and the infringement of that right by "B" will cause no loss to "A" but will remove some harm or even bring a benefit to "B", then the infringement of "A's" right by "B" may be excused and "B" acquires a legal right (15 *Israel L Rev* 49, 1980). He applies this principle to the neighborhood situation which may constitute an invasion of privacy, to wit:

''B'' constructs a window in a wall, which window overlooks the adjoining courtyard of ''A''; if ''B's'' window constitutes an invasion of ''A's'' privacy, then ''B'' may not construct the window, *unless*, according to the ''kofin'' principle, there is *no* possibility of present or future annoyance to ''A,'' such as ''B's'' use of a telescope for spying on ''A's'' courtyard! In this case the benefit to ''B'' of light and air must be denied and the ''kofin'' principle rejected since there is a possibility of invading the privacy of the owner of the adjoining courtyard. Thus, the general rule under Jewish law is that a neighbor may not construct a window in his wall which would overlook an adjoining courtyard since this would be an invasion of the privacy of the owner of the courtyard. (However, one may construct a window which is very high, since, because of its height, there will be no overlooking into the courtyard and no invasion of privacy.) This legal principle of ''kofin al midat S'dom'' is founded on a theory

—not surprising for a legal system based on religious law which abounds with moral and equitable commands—that even where one does not have a legal right, he can acquire one on the basis of ''kofin.'' Looking at this from the standpoint of the subservient party, the ''kofin'' rule overrides one's legal rights where insisting on exercising them brings him no benefit and waiving them in a specific situation would be beneficial to another. Although the ''kofin'' principle is much wider than the contemporary abuse of rights rules, perhaps because of this sweeping principle, Jewish law was constantly on guard to protect against its abuse. On the other hand, ''kofin'' is almost all-encompassing. It can alter contractual obligations; it can be applied not only to allay a possible damage but also to allow for a benefit or even a monetary profit; real property of another can be impinged on and there is even a minority view that another's property may be occupied against the owner's will; even physical changes in another's property may be made on the basis of ''kofin.'' But, the other side of the coin is one of strict adherence to the rule that ''kofin'' can never be resorted to where the subservient party would suffer some loss.

According to Dr. Shilo:

A major halakhic school of thought holds that the possibility of putting economic pressure on another is not of Sodomite character, and therefore ''kofin'' is *not* to be applied. Even if there is no loss or inconvenience there are other barriers, such as the majority view's negative attitude to squatting on another's property against the owner's will, even if his refusal to allow the squatting is arbitrary. Another safeguard against too wide an application of ''kofin'' is the rule that one cannot be forced to sell his property even if he has no need for it whatsoever, and another is in dire need of it. Also, it seems that a defense against a claim based on ''kofin'' will be accepted if the defendant shows that the plaintiff demanding the equitable ''kofin,'' had, in the past, acted inequitably toward the defendant. Equity will not follow inequity.

To illustrate further the complexity of this problem of privacy in Jewish law, Dr. Shilo goes back to the writings of the classic responsum and delineates what Rashba (R. Solomon ibn Aderet of Spain, 1235–1310), Rivash (R. Isaac ben Sheset of Spain and North Africa, 1326–1407), and Rosh (R. Asher ben Yehiel of Germany and Spain, 1250–1327) had to say on privacy. Rashba decided in favor of enjoining "B" from constructing the window because of the possibility that "A" might have to fight a case in court in the future in order to compel "B" to close up his window if "A" decided to build on his premises. Rashba points out that "A's" fears are logical, and "A" is not acting in the matter of the Sodomites. There is no need for "A" to be constantly forced to protect against "B's" window in order to be sure that "B" would not acquire a right to light and air over the years that the window remained open through undisturbed possession. Rashba also rejected a written guarantee from "B" that, as soon as "A" would build on his premises, "B" would close up his window. Rashba was worried about the burden upon "A" to keep the document of guarantee safe from loss as well as the need to watch over the document for so many years so that "A" would not forfeit his legal right. On the other hand, Rosh expressed a view on slightly changed facts, to wit: "A" has built a slanted roof on his house, and "B" constructs a window since there is no fear of invading the privacy of "A" since "people do not usually spend time on a slanted roof!" Therefore Rosh applied the "kofin" principle because there was no fear of a possible loss by "A" from "B's" window. Although Rivash agrees with Rosh's reasoning, Rivash comes to a different conclusion, to wit:

> One can acquire a right to open a window overlooking another's property even though it was kept open under legal circumstances which did not allow protest—if the window was kept open enough years. If this is the law concerning the right to light, then the owner of the roof has something substantial to fear—the possibility of the owner of the adjoining property's acquiring a right to construct windows which overlook his property. If so, a loss is possible, and therefore "kofin" should *not* be applied.

Rivash would enjoin the opening of the window which overlooks an adjoining slanted roof. Note that Rosh also rejects the possible arugment that the owner of the window may eventually acquire a legal right to open his windows which overlook his neighbor's property due to the rules of prolonged uninterrupted use, i.e., keeping his windows open, thus causing a loss to his neighbor, whose property will now be subject to an easement:

> Such an easement could cause harm or inconvenience to the home-owner with the slanted root if in the future he would want to make alterations in his building and remove the slanted roof. So long as one may not legally protest against the windows, no easement can be created—no matter how long the windows are kept open. An easement can be created only where one can legally protest against the developing easement, but does not do so. . . . Since no easement can be created, there is no fear of a possible loss. . . . Hence, the owner of the window benefits, the owner of the roof suffers no loss, ergo—"kofin."

The Israeli writer Carol Farhi (supra), in determining that the Israeli law of privacy derived from American legal development, accorded special recognition to a 1960 New York decision, Shapiro v. Health Insurance Co. (163 NE2d 333), which concerned the ''fairness'' of the information gathered and disclosed against an individual in order to determine whether the plaintiff surgeon was fit to serve on a medical panel; plaintiff surgeon contended that the information cited two malpractice cases against him but made no mention of the 1,800 successful surgeries that he had performed. The data also included the fact that he had been dropped from the staff of some hospitals but excluded a listing of his present important hospital affiliations. But the New York court found no breach of privacy because there was no malice, and a reasonable effort to ascertain the truth had been made by the defendants. Still another Israeli writer, Dr. Ruth Gavison, went a step further and posed the question whether there should be a general right of privacy in Israel (12 *Israel L Rev* 155, 1972). Her argument was based upon the fact that in 1972 Israel ''had not provided effective legal remedies for individuals injured in this way.''

It was not until 1981 that Israel enacted a protection of privacy statute (see Appendix herein), making it a crime to copy, publish, or read private correspondence of any citizen (including government officials) without the citizen's consent. This statute unfortunately was born of the government's anger over the media's success in uncovering scandals among Israeli government officials; the statute speaks of privacy in terms of spying on a person's activities, of publishing a photograph of someone in public life under circumstances which could be degrading, of reproducing the contents of a letter without permission of the sender or recipient, or of using a person's name, picture, or voice without permission for commercial purposes. On February 21, 1981, the *Jerusalem Post* editorialized:

> Unfortunately the protection it offers would be effective against only one potential ''invader'': the press (or the media in general). It is the press, and the press alone—but not government authority, that will not be able lawfully to make use of, say, the correspondence of private citizens (including government officials) without their permission—unless it could prove in court a ''public interest'' in publishing the material, or a ''legal, moral, social, or professional obligation to do so.'' These defenses are not likely to help a reporter or his editor except in an exceedingly ''liberal'' court. Government officials, on the other hand, are allowed to pry into the privacy of citizens so long as they come clothed with some legal authority, which should not be too difficult to obtain. The security agencies enjoy blanket defense for their brand of invasion of privacy under the new law. Indeed the law may be said to have made a citizen's privacy even more vulnerable than before to violation by constituted authority, whose power is immeasurably greater than that of the press.

Subsequently the Israeli statute on invasion of privacy was amended, and Section 18 (2) (b) was inserted: ''It will be a good defense that the invasion of privacy was done in circumstances in which the person who committed the act had the legal, moral, social or professional obligation to do so." This obvious weakness in the criminal law statute of privacy may very well undermine even the civil concept of privacy in Israel.

6.4 SOVIET UNION RECOGNITION OF PRIVACY

The Soviet Union, despite its dismal record of violations of human rights, professes in the Soviet Constitution to respect the right of privacy. Article 56 of the Constitution, for example, declares that "the privacy of citizens, and of their correspondence, telephone conversations, and telegraphic communications is protected by law." Article 57 continues by asserting that "respect for the individual and protection of the rights and freedoms of citizens are the duty of all state bodies, public organizations and officials. Citizens of the USSR have the right to protection by the courts against encroachments on their honor and reputation, life and health, and personal freedom and property." The sobering fact of reality, however, is found in Article 59, which reminds the Soviet citizen that he or she is "obliged to observe the Constitution of the USSR and Soviet laws, comply with the standards of socialist conduct, and uphold the honor and dignity of Soviet citizenship." Whether that leaves any room for respect for individual privacy is questionable, for under Article 39 the Soviet citizen is again reminded that "enjoyment by citizens of their rights and freedoms must not be to the detriment of the interests of society or the state or infringe upon the rights of other citizens."

In the November 1980 edition of *Soviet Life* magazine, which is circulated in the United States, an interview was conducted with Dr. Yelena Lukasheva, a longtime student of human rights, and Pyotr Oleinik, Deputy Minister of Internal Affairs. After Dr. Lukasheva defined "human rights" as including "the freedoms directly related to a person's right to protection against arbitrary interference in his or her private affairs, the inviolability of the home, privacy of correspondence, freedom of conscience, protection of the family, the fight to freedom of movement within the country and abroad, and so on," Oleinik continued:

> Soviet law considers human life to be of supreme value and encourages truly humane relations among people. This is how we understand the principles of human rights. "Respect for the individual and protection of the rights and freedoms of citizens are the duty of all state bodies, public organizations, and officials," reads the Soviet Constitution.
>
> Whom should the life, honor and dignity of citizens be protected against? First of all, against criminal elements, of which, regrettably, there are some. Our legal code regards premeditated murder as a most dangerous crime. To prevent it, the law provides for extensive crime prevention and prohibits the free sale of any weapons except hunting weapons. Even these sales are strictly regulated and supervised.

Oleinik answered a question about searches, letter-reading, and phone tapping:

Inviolability of the home in the USSR is also guaranteed by the Constitution: "No one may, without lawful grounds, enter a home against the will of those residing in it." A search can only be made after the start of criminal proceedings, when the investigating officer has good reason to believe that there are lawbreakers, weapons or stolen goods on the premises. But even in that case the law demands a well-founded request of the investigating officer which is backed by an attorney. If any delay might hamper the investigation, a search can be effected without an attorney's warrant, but then the attorney must be notified about this in writing within 24 hours.

The law contains similar provisions protecting the privacy of correspondence, cables and telephone conversations. Correspondence can be seized on the warrant of an attorney or by a court decision, but only if a crime has been committed and free correspondence between the accused persons or suspects might hinder the investigation.

I should add that illegal searches and any idle curiosity about the correspondence or phone calls of citizens, either by private persons or officials, are considered a crime and are severely punished by a long prison term.

It would appear that, on the basis of the international record, the USSR merely pays lip-service to these high ideals, for there are thousands and thousands of Soviet citizens who simply have no such rights, particularly the right to emigrate from the Soviet Union, much less the right of privacy.

6.5 INTER-AMERICAN RECOGNITION OF PRIVACY

The American Declaration of the Rights and Duties of Man (1948) and the American Convention of Human Rights are examples of Inter-American recognition of the right of privacy. The Declaration was adopted by the Ninth International Conference of American States, held in Bogota, Colombia, from March 30 to May 2, 1948, and therefore antedates the Universal Declaration of Human Rights adopted by the United Nations. The Convention adopted in 1969 did not enter into force until July 17, 1978, although the Inter-American Commission on Human Rights has been in operation since 1960.

The Declaration in Article 13 reads:

Every person has the right to take part in the cultural life of the community, to enjoy the arts and to participate in the benefits that result from intellectual progress, especially scientific discoveries.

He likewise has the right to the protection of his moral and material interests as regards his inventions or any literary, scientific or artistic work of which he is the author.

The provision that "everyone has duties to the community" in Article 29 of the Universal Declaration of Human Rights (adopted by the United Nations on December 10, 1948) finds its counterpart in the American Declaration, which also places equal emphasis upon rights and duties by dividing into two chapters, the first dealing with "rights" and the second with "duties." The Inter-

American Commission on Human Rights created by the Organization of American States has authority since 1965 to act on individual petitions complaining of violations of certain rights provided for in the American Declaration.

The American Convention of Human Rights (unlike the American Declaration, which under Article 22 states that "every person has a right to associate with others to promote, exercise and protect his legitimate interests of a political, economic, religious, social, cultural, professional, labor union or other nature") takes a broader view, as set forth in Article 16, which provides:

1. Everyone has the right to associate freely for ideological, religious, political, economic, labor, social, cultural, sports, or other purposes.
2. The exercise of this right shall be subject only to such restrictions established by law as may be necessary in a democratic society, in the interest of national security, public safety or public order, or to protect public health or morals or the rights and freedoms of others.
3. The provisions of this article do not bar the imposition of legal restrictions, including even deprivation of the exercise of the right of association on members of the armed forces and the police.

It is evident that these provisions make explicit what is implicit in other transnational prescriptions and that their protection extends to a wider range of groups specialized to the shaping and sharing of different values. Article 11 of the American Convention takes it a step further:

1. Everyone has the right to have his honor respected and his dignity recognized.
2. No one may be the object of arbitrary or abusive interference with his private life, his family, his home, or his correspondence, or unlawful attacks on his honor or reputation.
3. Everyone has the right to the protection of the law against such interference or attacks.

The very Preamble to the American Convention states that "the essential rights of man are not derived from one's being a national of a certain State, but are based upon attributes of the human personality." Article 1 then spells out the fact that

> [t]he States Parties to this Convention undertake to respect the rights and freedoms recognized herein and to ensure to all persons subject to their jurisdiction the free and full exercise of those rights and freedoms, without any discrimination for reasons of race, color, sex, language, religion, political or other opinion, national or social origin, economic status, birth, or any other social condition. And, for the purposes of this Convention, "person" means every human being.

However, an "alien" is given a different status, as shown in Article 22 (6), which reads: "An alien lawfully in the territory of a State Party to this Convention may be expelled from it only pursuant to a decision reached in accordance with law." Article 22 (8) stipulates:

In no case may an alien be deported or returned to a country, regardless of whether or not it is his country of origin, if in that country his right to life or personal freedom is in danger of being violated because of his race, nationality, religion, social status, or political opinions.

And Article 22 (9) states that "the collective expulsion of aliens is prohibited." But, in sharp contrast to "nationals," Article 22 (5) declares that "no one can be expelled from the territory of a state of which he is a national or be deprived of the right to enter it," and Article 23 further distinguishes the rights of aliens from the rights of nationals:

1. Every citizen shall enjoy the following rights and opportunities:

    a. to take part in the conduct of public affairs, directly or through freely chosen representatives;

    b. to vote and to be elected in genuine periodic elections, which shall be by universal and equal suffrage and by secret ballot that guarantees the free expression of the will of the voters; and

    c. to have access, under general conditions of equality, to the public service of his country.

2. The law may regulate the exercise of the rights and opportunities referred to in the preceding paragraph only on the basis of age, nationality, residence, language, education, civil and mental capacity, or sentencing by a competent court in criminal proceedings.

Indeed, the principal thrust is to accord nationals the same protection formerly accorded only to aliens, while at the same time raising the standard of protection for all human beings, nationals as well as aliens.

The American Convention on Human Rights is uplifting in the sense of dedication and commitment, as illustrated by Article 26, which provides:

The States Parties undertake to adopt measures, both internally and through international cooperation, especially those of an economic and technical nature, with a view to achieving progressively, by legislation or other appropriate means, the full realization of the rights implicit in the economic, social, educational, scientific, and cultural standards set forth in the Charter of the Organization of American States as amended by the Protocol of Buenos Aires.

And Article 29 is even more elaborate:

No provision of this Convention shall be interpreted as:

(a) permitting any State Party, group, or person to suppress the enjoyment or exercise of the rights and freedoms recognized in this Convention or to restrict them to a greater extent than is provided for herein;

> (b) restricting the enjoyment or exercise of any right or freedom recognized by virtue of the laws of any State Party or by virtue of another Convention to which one of the said states is a party;
>
> (c) precluding other rights or guarantees that are inherent in the human personality or derived from representative democracy as a form of government; or
>
> (d) excluding or limiting the effect that the American Declaration of the Rights and Duties of Man and other international acts of the same nature may have.

Article 30 also has general provisions about accommodations, to wit:

> The restrictions that, pursuant to this Convention, may be placed on the enjoyment or exercise of the rights or freedoms recognized herein may not be applied except in accordance with laws enacted for reasons of general interest and in accordance with the purpose for which such restrictions have been established;

as does Article 32:

> 1. Every person has responsibilities to his family, his community, and mankind.
> 2. The rights of each person are limited by the rights of others, by the security of all, and by the just demands of the general welfare, in a democratic society.

But the American Convention in Article 27 contains a derogation clause:

> In time of war, public danger, or other emergency that threatens the independence or security of a State Party, it may take measures derogating from its obligation under the present Convention to the extent and for the period of time strictly required by the exigencies of the situation, provided that such measures are not inconsistent with its other obligations under international law and do not involve discrimination on the ground of race, color, sex, language, religion, or social origin.

Appendix

ISRAEL PROTECTION OF PRIVACY LAW BILL

Prohibition of violation of privacy

1. No person shall violate the privacy of another.

Definition of violation of privacy

2. Violation of privacy includes:
(1) the investigation, surveillance and harassment of another;
(2) the listening-in or recording of the conversation of another without his knowledge by mechanical or electronic means or other devices, excluding a medical device which serves to raise a sound above its normal level;
(3) the photographing of a person or thing on private property;
(4) the photographing of a person in a public place or the publication of his photograph in circumstances under which the photograph or publication is liable to cause him embarrassment;
(5) the reading of a letter or a copy thereof without permission of the addressee or the person who sent it;
(6) the reading of written matter not intended for publication, or the use of its contents;
(7) the use of a person's name, appellation, picture or voice for profit-making or political activities;
(8) the breach of a duty of secrecy regarding the private affairs of a person which is prescribed by law;
(9) the breach of a duty of secrecy regarding the private affairs of a person which is prescribed by express or implied agreement;

(10) the use or passing-on of knowledge of the affairs of a person for a purpose other than that for which it was imparted;
(11) the publication or passing-on of any thing obtained by a violation of privacy under paragraphs (1) to (8) and (10).

Definition of publication

3. For the purposes of this Law, "publication" has the meaning it bears in section 2 of the Prohibition of Defamation Law, 5725-1975.

Violation of privacy a civil wrong

4. A violation of privacy is a civil wrong, and the provisions of the Civil Wrong Ordinance (New Version) [1968] shall apply thereto subject to the provisions of this Law.

Violation of privacy an offense

5. A person who wilfully violates the privacy of another in one of the ways specified in paragraphs (1) to (8), (10) and (11) of section 2 is liable to imprisonment for six months.

Trifling acts

6. No right to a civil or criminal claim or action shall arise under this Law in respect of a violation which is insubstantial.

Defences

7. In civil or criminal proceedings for violation of a privacy, it shall be a good defence if
(1) the injured party expressly or by implication consented to the violation;
(2) the violation was committed by a person bound to commit it under law or in pursuance of the direction of an authority duly competent in that respect or by permission of an authority as aforesaid;
(3) the violation was committed by a publication protected under section 13 of the Prohibition of Defamation Law, 5725-1965;
(4) the defendant committed the violation in good faith in one of the following circumstances—
(a) he did not know nor should have known of the possibility of a violation of the privacy of another,
(b) the violation was committed in circumstances under which a legal, moral or social duty lay upon the defendant to commit it,
(c) the violation was committed for the protection or advancement of a legitimate personal interest of the defendant,
(d) the violation was committed in the lawful conduct of the defendant's business or in the course of his normal work, provided that it was not committed by publication,
(e) a public interest was involved in the violation, justifying it in the circumstances of the case,
(f) the violation was by means of a photograph taken in public and the image of the injured party appears therein incidentally, or by the publication of such a photograph,

(g) the violation was committed by a publication protected under paragraphs (3) to (11) of section 15 of the Prohibition of Defamation Law, 5725-1965.

Burden of proof 8. (a) Where the defendant proves that he committed the violation in one of the circumstances mentioned in section 7(4) and that the violation did not go beyond the reasonable limits of such circumstances, he is presumed to have committed the violation in good faith.

(b) The defendant is presumed to have committed the violation not in good faith if he intended to do so to an extent beyond that which was reasonably necessary for the purpose of the matters for which a defense is provided under section 7(4).

(c) A defendant pleading a defence under section 7(4)(d) is presumed to have committed the violation not in good faith if he did so in the course of a breach of the rule of professional ethics applicable to him by virtue of law, or customary in his profession.

The State 9. This Law shall apply to the State subject to the provisions of sections 3 and 5 of the Civil Wrongs (Liability of the State) Law, 5712-1952.

Public Bodies 10. State authorities, local authorities and other bodies carrying out public functions in pursuance of law may, in so far as the same is not prohibited by any enactment, exchange information for the purpose of implementing any enactment or for any purpose within the powers or functions of the body passing on or receiving the information. The Minister of Justice may make regulations regarding the procedure for exchange of information as aforesaid.

Death of injured party 11. (a) No civil claim or criminal complaint under this Law shall be entertained for a violation of the privacy of a deceased person unless the claim or complaint was lodged during his lifetime and his relatives have within six months after the death notified the Court of their desire to continue prosecuting the claim or complaint. Nothing in the provisions of this section shall prevent the conviction of a person on a charge lodged on behalf of the State.

(b) For the purpose of this section, "relative" means a spouse, child or parent or, where the deceased left no spouse, child or parent [him surviving], a brother or sister.

Prescription 12. The period of prescription of a civil action in respect of which no claim has been lodged under this Law shall be two years.

Application of Prohibition of Defamation Law 13. The provisions of sections 21 and 22 of the Prohibition of Defamation Law, 5725-1965, shall *mutatis mutandis* apply to legal proceedings for a violation of privacy.

Special relief	14.	**The Court may in addition to any other relief order a person who has violated the privacy of another (1) to publish at his own expense the decision of the Court; (2) to deliver up to the injured party all the violating matter.**
Matter invalid as evidence	15.	**Matter obtained during a violation of privacy shall be inadmissible as evidence in court without the consent of the injured party unless the defendant has a defence under this Law or the Court gives leave to make use of the matter.**
Amendment of Civil Wrongs Ordinance	16.	**Section 34A of the Civil Wrongs Ordinance is repealed.**
Amendment of Criminal Procedure Law	17.	**In the Schedule of the Criminal Procedure Law, 5725-1965, after paragraph 12 there shall be added "(13) Offences against the Protection of Privacy Law."**
Saving of law	18.	**The provisions of this Law do not derogate from the provisions of any other law.**

Protection of Privacy Bill, *reprinted in* Elman, *Comment on the Kahn Committee Report on the Protection of Privacy,* 12 ISRAEL L. REV. 172, 176-79 (1977) (footnotes omitted) (brackets in original).

Index to Cases

Subject Index

About the Author

WARREN FREEDMAN, a member of the New York, Federal, and U.S. Supreme Court bars, served as corporate counsel to Bristol-Myers Company for 20 years in addition to his private law practice. He is the author of *International Products Liability* (3 vols.), *Products Liability for Corporate Counsels, Controllers, and Product Safety Executives, Allergy and Products Liability,* and *Richards on Insurance,* as well as two travel books and three sociology textbooks. Over the years he has contributed extensively to various law journals and reviews. He has taught on the graduate level at Rutgers University School of Law and the New School for Social Research.